Joe & Esther,

RAISED BY THE FBI

SCOTT SOMMER

Thank for your
long-standing support +
partnership. Blessings +
Best wishes!

"Some kids grow up pretending they are secret agents. Scott Sommer had a front-row seat to the FBI every day. He shares the story of his father's career along with the truth the Bible teaches about being a person of virtue. Using examples from Joseph, Moses, David, and others Sommer helps readers understand that character matters and God uses the circumstances of life to form our character."

John Byron, Ph.D
Dean of the Seminary & Professor of New Testament
Ashland Theological Seminary

RAISED BY THE FBI

IngramSpark

Scripture quotations are from the NEW AMERICAN STANDARD BIBLE, 1995 and the HOLY BIBLE: NEW LIVING TRANSLATION, 2015. Used with permission.

Cover Design by Cody Buriff, Scott Sommer & Chel Kissler. Creative layout by kreativityinc.com

ACKNOWLEDGEMENTS

*T*hank you to all who contributed to this book in some way. Especially, Bob Frederick who shared with my mom and dad how to have a personal relationship with Jesus, Bay Presbyterian Church, which has been a blessing and stalwart to our family for 37 years, Dave Drab, who gave the original idea to work my dad's stories into a devotional, Frank Figliuizzi for visiting us on that difficult day, and for his editing and publishing help, John Kane for his friendship with Dad for so many years and introducing us to deer hunting, along with Tom Lattanzi, who provided the location (It gave us so much father/son time), Jerry Personen and other FBI Cleveland agents and support staff who made an impression on my life, including Thalia Ventouris and Ernie Germany, who blessed me with their fond memories of Dad, Linda DeCredico for taking our calls, Sara Pachinger who supported Dad at HIDTA, Stu Shoaf for telling me to stay out of his underwear :) Rob Kirwan, who talked some sense into me, John Kirkland, John Kane, Dave Drab, Matt Hoke, Dan Leeper, Chris Garnett, Jerry Viola and others who gave me details on stories and cases, Jennifer Hoffman and Amarra Oriaku who read the first drafts and did the original editing, Drew Gittins who gave input on organization, Travis Fielder, Jon Christianson and Dave McCracken who gave an agent's perspective, Dr. John Byron, gave the impetus to include stories of biblical characters, the faculty of Ashland Theological Seminary for expanding my thinking and helping me draw closer to Jesus, Marie McGaha for believing in me and giving me a chance to become a published author, The Sommer, Decker, Arkangel, Krisak and Carter families for being a part of dad's life, Mom, Sarah and Jenny- we lived this story together, Big-Ryan, Scrubbles, Glorio and Mittens-Ellen for inspiring me to be a good father, Emily, the greatest life-partner and teammate ever, and for being forced to read when I needed help.

For Ryan, Anna, Ben, CJ, Jack, Ellen, Brynn, Luke, Nolan, Annalise and Skye

You didn't get a chance to know Grandpa, but I know he can't wait to know you.

You have an excellent name

PROVERBS 22:1

INTRODUCTION
HOW WE'RE RAISED

We are all raised by someone. I was raised by the Federal Bureau of Investigation. That's right. The FBI. Metaphorically of course- they don't have a nursery in the J. Edgar Hoover building.

My parents also raised me, but the FBI was an inseparable part of my childhood and meaningfully shaped who I am today. I've never lived with the FBI not being a part of my life. The FBI provided the income for our family as I was growing up. It supports my mom today. Today, I'm an FBI Chaplain, and now I'm writing a book about the FBI. Geez, I can't get away from the thing.

I started compiling stories from my dad's career after he died unexpectedly twelve years ago so the grandkids would remember him. As I did this, I realized most of the stories revolved around life lessons, character virtues, doing the right thing, and faith.

I have been fascinated and compelled by the idea of character most of my adult life. My favorite books consist of inspiring biographies of famous people who faced down difficulty and hardship, prevailing in the end. In my college years, the lack of character in my own life led me down a path of terrible choices, brokenness, and emotional break-down. When I finally reached the end of myself, I surrendered to God and sensed Him inviting me into a new, rich life of adventure and fulfillment as a follower of Christ; one far more compelling and fulfilling than my previous one. When I graduated from college, I became a minister, which may have been God's payback for my earlier antics.

One of the greatest things I learned growing up is what a person of character looks like. A great deal of this came from being raised by my dad, an FBI Special Agent for thirty years and the organization he worked for. I spent a lot of time around other agents and support staff. They were always kind and affirming, genuinely excited to interact with me. There was something different about them, but I couldn't put my finger on it. It rubbed off on me. They built up my self-esteem as a young boy. I figured those important people liked me, so I must have been pretty cool. I grew up confident.

In this book, I've related stories from my dad's FBI career I either lived through personally or was raised hearing from my dad and others. I also present snapshots from the lives of biblical characters who demonstrated character and faith in their lives- or not. I grew up going to Sunday school and I was captivated by the stories of adventure, courage, failure, and faith that I found in the Bible. They stuck with me as a kid and shaped me as an adult.

Then I will draw out an ethical or moral principle for us to ponder. There's a lot of lessons about God I will relate as well, but as a minister, you knew that was coming. Hey, at least this isn't a bait and switch.

I've addressed a few areas of interest to church and ministry leaders such as interpretation of scripture and church strategy.

As a Christian, I believe character and God are inseparable because moral authority informs our character virtue. That higher authority declares what character and morality are and are not. It's how we know right from wrong. God claims to be that authority.

If we don't believe that is true, we become our own arbiters of morality, regardless of which social or philosophical system we adhere. This is difficult because as we know, human beings aren't perfect. Our standards of morality can and have changed, and are sometimes even optional, making them less trustworthy. Additionally, living lives of character is how we please God, and we all sense a desire to please someone. Our innate belief in a just and loving higher power gives us the opportunity to be good people, which also gives us happiness and satisfaction. Deep inside, we want to do good. If we exist by random mutation, it seems peculiar to find these propensities in our hearts- unless we are meant for more.

This presents a problem for the Naturalist. Character is not opportune for a life governed by natural selection. That is, if self-preservation is primary, it's hard to see kindness, sacrifice and putting others first as beneficial for individual survival. Those traits would be liabilities. Some might argue a species inherently knows it's in the best interest of itself to do good, but that seems to be calling on an ancillary and external logic- something more than just a survival instinct. You've just moved out of pure naturalism and made an appeal to something outside of science. You've just proved the Theist's point—there's something else out there.

The Secular Humanist has a similar obstacle. Though they affirm character and intrinsic goodwill toward others, they are faced with two problems. The first is the origin itself of character in a natural world- where does it come from? Why would we want to do good in a survival-of-the-fittest world? The second is motivation. If there is no God and no afterlife, why should we be motivated to do anything good? Why deny ourselves the pleasure that comes from being purely humanistic and following our own natural desires? Occultist Aleister Crowley understood this, and in his creed called it: "Do what thou wilt."[1] The Humanist's solution is that we do good simply because it's the right thing to do, but there is no answer for who or what decided what was good in the first place. Once again, there's something else operating here outside the system's paradigms.

Eastern Spiritualists also must do some tap dancing. They allow for a transcendent, universal power. Our life energy makes all living (and maybe inanimate) things a part of that power. Karma and reincarnation is the moral reward/punishment system that governs this universal power or life force. This allows for a motivation to do good, but it also obligates you to believe in an arbiter of good: an authoritative moral agent who manages the application of karma and reincarnation. Who or what is that? Who decides you become a bug if you're bad and get Moksha/Nirvana if you're good?

God offers a durable and resolute foundation for character virtue in our lives. God's authority explains our knowledge of good and evil. God makes us in His image which gives us the desire to do good, and God's promise of eternal life gives us motivation to carry out the good. God is the something else that's out there.

Whew. Okay I'm done. If it sounds like I'm trying to convince you that Theism is the best world view, and to believe and follow God, I am! If you don't have a belief or relationship with God that anchors your character, I truly hope this book might be that catalyst. If you are a Christian, I hope this book stirs you to follow God with strength and passion, and go forth to change the world for good. But regardless of who you are, whatever your beliefs may be or wherever your personal character is at this time, I pray you will find these pages enjoyable, affirming and inspiring.

LET'S START OUR JOURNEY.

CHAPTER ONE
DAD

I was born in Washington, D.C. My family moved three times before I turned five. Agents understand that well. Our home phone number was always unlisted, and my diaper bag contained diapers, wipes, an extra pacifier, and my dad's .38 Chief's Special revolver and credentials when he was babysitting. You should've seen the pediatrician's face when I had an accident during a checkup, and he reached inside the bag for a wipe.

"Whoa! You don't see that every day!" he exclaimed as he peered at the gun in between the Desitin and the wet wipes.

My father, John B. Sommer, began his career as a lab technician in 1970, becoming an expert in shoe footprint, fingerprint, handwriting identification, and gaining a master's degree in forensic science. He also gave tours of the J. Edgar Hoover building and FBI headquarters. He qualified to become an agent in 1972. In his field offices, he served as the resident expert in evidence and crime scene management, working the infamous 1989 kidnapping case of Amy Mihajevic in Cleveland, Ohio, which remains unsolved. He created the Evidence Response Team in the Cleveland division, which is now an FBI specialty team across the country. He worked his entire career in the organized crime squads of the offices he was assigned, focusing on the Sicilian Mafia crime families, also known as *La Cosa Nostra* (translated in English as "Our Thing").

The '70s and '80s were a volatile time for the mob nationally, and my dad, along with a squad of talented agents, was able to play a key role in its local dismantling and eventual demise in Cleveland. He worked such notorious and important cases as Danny Greene, Jackie Presser and the Teamsters, Ray "Luc" Lavasseur, Angelo "Big Ange" Lonardo and mob boss James "Jack White" Licavoli. In his final years with the FBI, my dad was the Supervisory Special Agent (SSA) for the organized crime squad working in public corruption and drug cases.

My dad was old school. He wore a blazer, tie, and a heavy stainless steel, Smith & Wesson Model 66 revolver to work every day. His car held a shotgun on a roof rack, a ballistic vest, an FBI raid jacket, and a forensic evidence collection kit. A police radio was on the dashboard and a magnetic roof siren light sat on the console. Once he turned the siren on when we were parked in front of a Convenient food mart, to my joy, and everyone in the store turned and looked out the window. In the glove box were several boxes of 00 buckshot shotgun ammo.

When I was in elementary school, my father possessed the *coolest* job amongst the other little boys, hands down. I was like a celebrity at recess. The kids heard my dad was an FBI agent, and I would hold court. They crowded around me, mouths hanging open, releasing a litany of questions:

"Whoa! How many bad guys has he arrested?"

"Does he wear sunglasses? Does he carry a gun? Can I see it?"

"Has he ever gone undercover?"

"What is his car like? Is it fast?"

Once, my dad gave a friend of mine his business card. It might as well have been a $100 bill from the look on his face. It was neat, I must say. As a young boy, it gave my confidence a boost knowing people thought my dad was so cool. He arrested many people in his career, he went undercover, and most of the time when I was younger, I had no idea what he was doing.

My dad taught me about life. Explicitly when he told me things, implicitly when I watched him. He shaped me, and I carry him with me today - but only the good stuff. Jokes aside, he also had many faults and wasn't perfect by any stretch. There are things about him I've chosen to avoid in my life that, because of nature and nurture, I have a propensity towards. But I did learn about character and its importance. Not only from him as he sought to live ethically, but by those he worked with and what he did as a career. How you act means something. What you say means something. What you think means something. How you treat others; it all means something.

Character development and what kind of person we become, at least initially, depends upon who raises us. Not all of us had good experiences growing up, not all of us can say we experienced positive values being taught or role models to follow, which is saddening. Sometimes the negative examples are stronger than the positive ones. I was blessed to be raised in a generally positive environment with character virtue being upheld and honored.

But what is a person with good character? Long-time counselor Larry Crabb offers a description:

"You know them when you see them. They give off a vibe, and often you notice them quickly. They might seem like they have it all together. They have confidence. They know what they're doing and where they're going. They seem different than others, like they're operating with a distinct set of rules, or they answer to an alternate source of authority. They act like they don't need our approval. They are kind and considerate, but they won't do something to jump through hoops. There is gentleness, but at the same time, a firmness. You can't push them around and they won't be manipulated. The truth is, they've already made up their mind about the most important things and they aren't about to change based on convenience. When they say they will do something, they do it. When they fail, they own it and admit their mistake. When we interact with them, we feel a calm and are put at ease. They open their mouth not to gossip or slander someone, but offer something profound, full of wisdom and generosity. Rarely do they complain, and when they do, they don't impugn another person's character. They radiate positivity, and we feel good when we're around them. We feel safe. We

want to spend time with them. And why? Because we want to be like them. They are who we want to be. "[2]

THAT'S A PERSON OF CHARACTER.

Can you resonate with this description? Is this talking about you or are you a million miles away? Do you wonder how you could become such a person, if ever? Do you want to be a better man or woman?

That's what this book is about.

I learned a lot about who I wanted to be from being raised by my dad and the FBI. Character is more caught than taught.

CHARACTER IS MORE CAUGHT THAN TAUGHT.

It's mercurial and sometimes difficult to describe, but it helps to have a working definition to start with. So, what is character, exactly? Well since it's my book, I'll suggest the following as a definition:

Good character consists of several traits easily recognizable by people in every time and culture. Among these are kindness, respect, courage, honesty, gratitude, perseverance and humility.

WE ADMIRE AND ASPIRE TO THESE TRAITS IN OUR LIVES.

Recently, some have called into question the good name of the FBI, but I can say with confidence that character virtue is what the Bureau has always striven for.

The Bureau has an official seal, with a list of traits that are an additional meaning for the FBI acronym.

FIDELITY, BRAVERY, INTEGRITY.

You can see them listed above in the middle of the seal.

These three words were chosen to typify to what the men and women of the FBI aspire.

I say aspire because I'm under no illusion that the FBI is perfect. No agency, no person, no organization is perfect, including the FBI. It's important to remember this because the current cultural environment seems to demand perfection, or face public shaming. But we have not, and will not achieve perfection as human beings. There must always be room for mistakes and being in-process. We extend each other forgiveness, and this builds trust. A good educator will tell you trust is essential for a viable environment of learning and growing. When something is healthy, an organization or a person, it grows, learns, and changes for the better. Every emotionally and mentally healthy person knows what good character is.

The FBI aspires to high ideals, and yet it has also made mistakes. As a result it has changed - and will change, for the better.

Early on as a kid, I realized that because my dad worked for the FBI, he had a unique kind of job. The job depended on being honest, brave, and doing the right thing. But not everyone appreciates these character traits, not everyone wants them to exemplify their life. And because of that, because of the nature of the job, I learned quickly there was always a chance, however slight, my dad might not come home from work at night. It hurt me to know there were people who hated my dad so much they wanted to kill him. Normal dads didn't have people that wanted to kill them. We all had a normal in our upbringing. This was my normal.

NORMAL DADS DIDN'T HAVE PEOPLE WHO WANTED TO KILL THEM.

Our normal meant daddy worked late at night and went away on "trips." My mom always told me, "Pray for daddy tonight." All I knew was it was dangerous. Years later, I learned just how dangerous the situations were—guarding mobsters with death warrants from assassins, executing armed raids, going undercover or arresting violent criminals. My dad fought against these bad guys to protect the rest of us.

My dad was a hero because he did the right thing.

My dad had character.

Here's his story.

CHAPTER TWO
PRISON RIOT

In 1973, the Vietnam War was winding down, leaving raw emotion and sharp divisions in our country. Motown, Classic Rock and Disco streamed through the radio waves. People were wearing bell-bottoms and saying things like "Groovy" and "Far out" and had way more hair than necessary. The '60s counterculture movement continued its profound influence, slowly driving the philosophical attitude of the United States from an optimistic modernism to a skeptical postmodernism, questioning and challenging truth and authority. The era of *Leave it to Beaver* was over.

My dad was a new FBI agent in the gritty, historical city of Philadelphia. He had an exciting new job and a new one-year-old son. Me. He wore a stiff polyester suit, huge tie, and sported some serious sideburns—there are pictures to prove it.

My dad and his partner had just finished interviewing an inmate at Holmesburg Prison in downtown Philadelphia. Built in 1896, this ancient, rock-hewn fortress once housed thirteen hundred of some of the city's most dangerous men as they paid their debts to society. Holmesburg was shut down in 1995, having been in continuous use for nearly one hundred years. Today, it's a decaying, eerie destination sought by ghost hunters. There's something ghastly about an abandoned prison. Maybe the past presence of so much evil amassed in one place, for decades upon decades. Or maybe terrible memories of broken lives, murder, and abuse. Even worse was the situation at Holmesburg. Prior to closing its doors, the prison gained a macabre reputation for conducting unethical dermatological experiments upon inmates. They had their skin doused with chemicals, infected with fungus, frozen, burned, then removed and studied by researchers. It was almost reminiscent of Josef Mengele, the notorious Auschwitz doctor of death. Long after the experiments concluded, a graduate student entered the prison to teach a literacy class. To his horror, inmates were covered in gauze and bandages, still suffering from the abusive practices.[3]

Back in '73 Holmesburg was in full swing and bustling with activity. Federal agents often paid visits to convicted criminals who were part of organized crime outfits. The inmate was brought to an interview room and the agents plunked down a big yellow legal pad on the desk and some type of awkward, strained conversation would occur. Usually, a mixture of mostly unhelpful, and one or two bits of helpful information for the agents. My dad and his partner met with the warden to give him an update on the interview. As they left the warden behind his heavy, solid wood desk, they felt hopeful with the bits of information they received. They were also a little bit relieved to be exiting the prison.

I can relate. I've spent a lot of time in prisons myself ministering to inmates, and it's essentially being locked up yourself for eight hours at a time. You cannot go where you want to go or walk where you want to walk. You ask to use the restroom. You stay with your escorts and movement is slow and deliberate. Once we're in there, we put on positive, encouraging programs for the inmates, talk about Jesus and pray for them. That part is great, but when it's time to go, I'm one of the first out the door. There's a vague sort of apprehension, I've noticed, as you're exiting a prison. You almost have the instinct to run for it, as if an alarm might sound at any moment and a corrections officer yells out, *"You! Stop right there!"* And you wouldn't be allowed to leave. Even though you haven't done anything wrong.

Or maybe I'm alone, here, and should have kept this to myself.

I will say I am genuinely grateful to walk out of the prison and back to my life of fresh air and freedom. I'm also ready for a shower. Prisons aren't known for their Autumn Fresh pot-pourri scent and Mr. Clean-certified facilities.

The agents began to make their way out of the prison. Faint echoes of yelling and raised voices bounced off the walls of the long, shiny hallways. Regular prison sounds. They reached the exit, and the dull, thick steel door buzzed and clicked open. The agents walked through the courtyard surrounded by thirty-five-foot-high stone walls, like a Medieval castle, menacing circles of razor wire adorning the top. That feeling of relief began, almost being back to freedom. With a spring in their step, they passed through the front entrance and made their way toward the parking lot. All was quiet now, no more echoes or metallic noises or buzzing. Birds chirped in the slight breeze of the spring air.

The agents felt the tension in their bodies release as they drove away. Ahh. Someone cracked a joke and smiled. Now they could relax.

But then, something happened that broke the silence.

The whine of multiple police sirens pierced ears. Appearing on the street horizon, numerous police cars began streaming toward the prison in full lights and sirens. You only see the lights first when they're coming from far away. Pulling to the side of the road to let them by, my dad switched on the police scanner and heard that a riot had begun in the prison at that exact moment. A few minutes after my father and his partner walked out of the prison, through the heavy door and courtyard, rioting inmates, full of rage and adrenaline entered the assistant warden's office and stabbed him in the throat with shanks—homemade knives made from sharpened pieces of plastic. As the assistant warden bled to death on the floor, the warden heard the commotion and ran into the adjoining room. He was brutally murdered as well.

This happening in the same room, in the same place my dad had stood just minutes earlier.

Minutes earlier. Not hours. Not days. Minutes.

Amazing.

But was it luck, chance, good Karma, or the guidance of a higher power? I don't personally believe in luck, chance, or Karma, but I do believe another Power was protecting my dad that day. My dad felt it.

As the prison-break siren slowly wound up and methodically droned through the air, the fortunate FBI agents sat stiffly in their car: dazed, confused, and staring into space. Then they looked at each other, first in shock, then in gratitude, then in guilt. The agents had been the last ones through the door before the riot began.

The first time I heard this story as a kid, it stopped me in my tracks. I couldn't believe what I heard.

"Mom, Daddy could have died?"

A lot would have been different if those inmates would have found two credential-carrying FBI agents in the warden's office that day. I probably would have grown up without a father.

The Apostle Paul from the New Testament also just made it out alive. An example of one of the most unlikely persons to

"MOM, DADDY COULD HAVE DIED?"

come to the Christian faith, Paul was a Pharisee, a member of an elite and powerful Jewish religious sect. He was educated and a Roman citizen, which meant high-end status in the Ancient Near East. He wasn't neutral towards Christians or simply didn't prefer them, he despised them. He made it his mission, for the glory of God, to hunt them down, drag them out of their homes, and place them in prison, separating families and destroying lives. He was so zealous he once volunteered to be the cloak-check guy for other Pharisees when they set them down to murder a Christian.

But then everything changed. While on his way to Damascus in Syria with orders to arrest even more Christians, Paul was immediately struck blind by God and heard the audible voice of Jesus. That would do it. For three days he stayed that way. During that time of solitude and darkness, Paul became a follower of Jesus. Shortly after, he completely regained his sight.

But recall Paul's personality—passionate, communicative, and hard-charging. He could not keep his newfound faith to himself. So he took to the streets and began telling every-

BUT THEN EVERYTHING CHANGED

one he could about Jesus—the very thing other Christians had done. Predictably, the Pharisees did not receive this well, and soon Paul was facing his own death threats. The Damascus Christians realized Paul was about to be murdered, so they found a large empty fruit basket and yelled at him to get in. Immersed in the aroma of fresh figs smashed beneath his sandals, Paul was lowered over the city wall and escaped into the night.

But Paul, like many of us, needed time for God to work on his brash ways before he was ready for more ministry opportunities. Thirteen years later after a time of solitude and character growth, Paul was sought out to become a full-time missionary. God used Paul mightily to build His kingdom. Most of our New Testament was authored by Paul, dictated to a scribe.

Can you think of a time when your life was in danger, or you almost experienced injury or serious negative financial or vocational consequences? Have you ever been let down in a basket? What was it for you? How do you characterize that? Is there a higher power guiding and directing our lives?

A seminary professor once said we are immortal until the time God has given us is up. Psalm 139:16 says it this way:

Your eyes have seen my unformed substance;
and in Your book were written all the days
that were ordained for me, When as yet
there was not one of them.

God ultimately controls our fate, but not just those who believe. Consider Ezekiel 18:5:

Behold, all souls are Mine; the soul of the father as well the soul of the son is Mine, The soul who sins will die.

God is in control of all our lives. The wardens who died that day, their families, my dad, and every person that has ever walked the face of the earth is under God's control. Yes, we have some measure of free will, but free will is also under God's control. Most people pray, and when we pray, we are asking God to exercise control over a circumstance, to intervene and save the day, and rightly so. Praying is a personal acknowledgment of God's overall power; a word Christians call sovereignty.

I don't remember it, but my dad came home that night from Holmesburg Prison, narrowly avoiding a deadly confrontation with men with nothing to lose. He played with me after dinner and helped put me down to bed in my crib. He had trouble getting to sleep that night. Later, he told me couldn't stop thinking about what had happened to him. Someone must have been pulling the strings.

It's not always easy, but I choose to believe in God's sovereignty. There's been too many crazy circumstances, too much coincidence. Too many times being the last one out the door. Too many times getting let down in a fruit basket.

Maybe you feel the same.

CHAPTER THREE
DEATH WARRANT

We can protect ourselves from what we can control. We may or may not feel a need for protection in our lives. Protection implies the existence of a potentially harmful force. Most of us realize that such forces are present in our lives, but we don't make the connection that we actively work to shield ourselves from these forces. We do this through wearing seatbelts, putting on sunscreen, buying life insurance policies, taking vitamins, getting new tires, locking our doors, and contributing to a 401K. These are all measures of protection and provision we take. We may call this simply being wise, but it's because of the negative possibilities that exist in the world. There are some things we need protection from.

Some things, like the Mafia.

The huge, boat-like '70s Cadillac crept along the street, moving through the shadows of the towering palm trees on the humid, clear night. Someone in the house killed the lights. Straining to see the license plate through the sheer drapes, the binoculars finally made it visible. Ohio. But which county? What is the writing on the license plate?

Cuyahoga county. Cleveland.

Silence.

"No way. It couldn't be. It couldn't."

The agents' hearts dropped into their stomachs. Beads of sweat formed on their foreheads as they peered through the darkened windows. Silence except for the car's tires crunching over downed and dried-up palm bark on the street. No one dared to move or speak or think. More silence. Sighs of disbelief and protest. Whispered cursing.

Crushing anxiety.

It's 1985, and the boss of the Cleveland Mafia, Anglo Lonardo, known as "Big Ange," has agreed to become a federal informant while serving time in prison. Several of Dad's colleagues had made it happen. In exchange for his testimony and information on other members, he was released. Once word got around the mob community that the elderly grandfather-type had become a snitch, he instantly became a marked man, destined for death. It was only a matter of time. A price of thousands of dollars in cash was placed on his head to anyone who killed him—a death warrant. It didn't matter what, how, or where, as long as the guy was dead. Quickly, he was relocated into FBI protective custody, twenty-four hours a day for eighteen months straight. My father was one of the agents regularly assigned to his protection detail.

Protective custody is stressful on everyone, the protected and those who are doing the protecting. It's probably hard to relax when people are trying to kill you. It was hard on the agents. They had to move every day or two, with their lone Mafioso prisoner in tow. They traveled to other states. Agents rotated in and out for duty, back and forth. Three days on, a day or two off. At times, my dad slept with his loaded .357 Magnum revolver next to his pillow like a teddy bear—when he was able to sleep.

It was a tough time for our family. Kids have that ability to sense tension in a home. My dad wasn't around very much. He was always gone, coming back for a few days at a time, eating, showering, shaving, washing clothes, then leaving again and never telling me or my sister what the heck he was doing. Judging by my mom's reaction, all I knew is that it had to do with bad guys, and it was *really* dangerous this time. We grew up with dangerous. It was part of the deal. FBI agents carry guns for a reason.

I can imagine now as an adult how nerve-wracking that

must have been for my poor mom. Talk about PTSD.

"Yeah, bye dear. I'm gonna go guard this guy that people are getting paid to kill. But don't worry, we hid him pretty well this time."

"Okay, call you in the morning! Have a good sleep!"

It's weird to think about. These FBI agents were willing to lay down their lives to protect a guy that had been a long-time enemy. Not exactly a nice guy, either. Murder had a way of running in Mafia families. Lonardo's own father had been murdered and Lonardo testified to a jury that he personally killed his father's murderer.

"I pulled out a gun and shot him", he said matter-of-factly at his trial.[4]

But regardless of the philosophical irony at play here, the FBI had one goal—protect this Mobster at all costs. Keep the guy alive. And not because they liked him, but because it was the morally right thing to do as a person of character. They weren't going to give up Lonardo without a fight. And it wouldn't be a Twitter feud. It would be an awful life or death struggle. People were going to die.

The Cadillac rolled on slowly past the darkened home. The agents slumped against the wall in relief. The danger was over, for the moment. But there was no telling what may happen next or if the car would come back with more cars and when, or even if the hiding place had been found out. The interminable minutes dragged by that night until the heartening and glorious morning sun pierced through the shades. Usually there's a depressing feeling when you see the morning light and you haven't slept yet. Not this time. It was beautiful. They had survived. The small band of agents and the geriatric Mafia boss evacuated as fast as their exhausted bodies were able.

PEOPLE WERE GOING TO DIE

What are the chances that a Cadillac with Ohio plates,

Cuyahoga county for that matter, would slowly drive past that particular house, many states, many hours away from Ohio, on that night, at that time? It could have been a vacationer, but more likely it was Mafia assassins.

How could it not have been?

Even weirder, why weren't they attacked that night? What stopped it? The agents never found out and didn't care to. They enthusiastically got out of there, happy to be alive.

They never saw that car again in those eighteen months.

I think they were being protected. My dad, the other agents, even the odious mobster were being protected. That's sure what my dad believed. Looking back, these two razor-close calls served to get his attention, causing him to think about what kind of person he was and evaluate his character. He wondered if he was being protected for a reason.

In Psalm 144:2, the writer says that God is his protection and *high tower*. A high tower was an essential part of protection for cities in the Ancient Near East, along with walls, where enemy invasion was always plausible. If you remember the Lord of the Rings and Hobbit movies, armies would lay siege to a city. They'd show up, surround the city and cut off inbound water and food supplies. Then they'd build siege ramps and siege towers, which were mobile ladders containing soldiers ready to jump over the walls when they got close. High towers provided defending archers places to fire at advancing siege engines, setting them on fire and killing enemy soldiers. The Psalmist that wrote about high towers was David from the Bible. The same person from David and Goliath fame. A little shepherd boy goes up against a 6'9" elite warrior (considered a giant in those times since the average male was about 5'5") armed only with a sling and a few stones. Goliath, bursting with pride and confidence, takes the bait. David slings his stone and unleashes a direct hit to the forehead of Goliath. The giant falls to the ground, shaking heaven and earth. David wins.

But rainbows and roses did not follow. King Saul, the

current king of Israel, became jealous of David's newfound popularity, feeling threatened. So he tried to use David for spear-throwing practice. David was forced to flee for his life.

David penned the following words while he was a fugitive on the run from King Saul, sleeping in caves, every night full of anxiety and exhaustion and little sleep.

Similar to protective custody, I imagine.

Saul was hunting him, seeking his death, all because David was more popular than he was. But David turned to God because he realized He was his true protection.

Do not fear, for I am with you. Do not anxiously look about you for I am your God. I will strengthen you. I will protect you, surely. I will uphold you with My righteous right hand.
ISAIAH 41:10

God offers that sense of ease and security we crave. God offers protection.

We are on a quest for it throughout our whole lives. Only one source can truly deliver. Deep inside, we know this. We may not trust God, follow God, or even like God, but many people acknowledge His existence and sovereignty, especially when they need protection. It's that "no athiests in a foxhole" maxim.

In the first year or two of my dad's career as a zealous young agent in Philadelphia, he made a foolish mistake. A bank robber had been cut by a broken window during his escape. My dad, along with local police and other reactive squad agents, began pursuing the wounded criminal by car, then by foot. It was easy to know where this guy was going: follow the blood trail. They tracked the bank robber to an abandoned house. But my dad, full of adrenaline, entered the house alone. With his drawn revolver in hand and his partner still exiting the car outside, he ran into the home quickly. Seeing an open window on the second floor at the top of the staircase, he bypassed multiple danger areas and dashed up the stairs. The blood trail ended at the open window which led outside to the fire escape. Drapes on the window, freshly smeared with blood, slowly swayed in the wind.

WHAT AM I DOING?

"What am I doing?" my dad said as he stood there in a stupor. "I could have been killed. Someone must have been looking out for me."

Protection.

CHAPTER FOUR
BAD GUYS

John Sommer, like all of us, was on a journey of self-discovery. He now believed that a higher power had a place and authority in his life. Intellectual ascent is one thing, but believing something influences or acts upon you personally, is another.

John was held back in elementary school because he was a poor reader. It was a wound he carried all his life. There was a newscaster that, whenever she came on TV, Dad would react with a visceral anger, because she reminded him of his reading teacher. Later in his life, they learned it wasn't because John didn't care about reading, it was that he had dyslexia. He was terrified of reading. In elementary school in the early '50s, the teacher thought the solution was to expose him to his fear, and often asked him to stand and read aloud. Snickers and laughter would accompany his presentation as he stumbled through the assignment. Probably not a great teaching strategy.

As an adult, reading was still a challenge for him, but he began to pick up his Bible to read about the God he saw in the world, the God he believed might be protecting him and others in his job. The Bible talked about real good and real evil in the world. That wasn't a problem for John. He saw evil every day.

He even talked to it.

"Quiet... all of you, quiet! Get upstairs now. You're dad's on the phone with a bad guy!"

It was after dinner one night in the early '80s. My sisters and I were playing before bedtime. It's that window of time for young families after dinner before it's time to get the little ones in the bathtub. For me as a father, it was a happy time roughhousing with my kids on the carpet and having fun. Wrestling, Nerf gun wars, Playmobil adventures. The impetus is to get their energy out before they go to bed. Admittedly, the strategy sometimes backfires and they get more wound up than before. Then my wife gets upset with me.

On that particular night the big, pastel-colored phone fixed on the kitchen wall rang. The FBI office was calling. My dad received a phone call from an informant that was about to be patched through from the switchboard. This informant was embedded in the Mafia and risking his life talking to the Feds. He was about to give out some names and numbers. Dad came into the kitchen and took the phone. He pulled out a big yellow legal pad ready to take notes.

My sisters and I continued laughing and playing, ignoring the order to go upstairs. Not that kids ever do that. Suddenly my mom became more intense, walking towards us, and yelling to get out of the room. She didn't want our voices heard in the background. We finally started going upstairs and into our rooms with the doors closed. My dad also headed upstairs, not knowing we were there as well. He picked up the phone in his bedroom and closed the door. My mom hung up the phone in the kitchen. All was quiet.

That was cutting-edge technology in those days.

I remember feeling scared, first by my mom's reaction and then by the whole bad-guy thing.

What is happening?

How bad is this guy?

Can he see my sisters and me through the phone?

An eerie silence saturated the house. A sense of expectancy hung in the air.

I've always been adventurous, or maybe rebellious, so defying orders I opened my door. I tip-toed over to my parents' bedroom and pressed my ear to the door. I heard my dad's voice, low and muffled, and then a pause. Then more. The conversation seemed serious, it was a scary thing for a kid to hear.

Was the bad guy talking about kids he had kidnapped?

Were any of them blonde-haired, 8-year-old boys with a bowl haircut?

I remember thinking my dad was brave. Whoa... he talked to bad guys, and he isn't even afraid! I was way too scared to even think about doing that. **Bad guy** was the term my parents used to describe the people my dad worked with or arrested- the kidnappers, murderers, bank robbers, Mafia members, and drug dealers. My dad dealt with them every day. He even talked to them in his own bedroom.

As I think about this impression now as an adult, there's an interesting question that surfaces: The term **bad guy**. It's just a catch-all word and I'll keep using it in this book. The connotation is scary, mean, evil people. Everyone knows what bad guys are.

But thinking philosophically for a minute, how do you really become a bad guy? How bad do you have to be to have your primary identifier be **bad**? I mean, when do you go from someone who's made some poor choices to being a bad guy?

The Bible answers this question for us succinctly. We're all bad guys according to God's standard. The text explains:

For all have sinned and fallen short of the glory of God.
ROMANS 3:23

There is none righteous, not even one.
ROMANS 3:10

According to the Bible, we are all bad guys. It may sound offensive because we like to consider ourselves inherently good on the inside. We like to think that people are basically good. But that isn't what the Bible says. And there are plenty of people out there who don't care about being good at all.

HOW BAD DO YOU HAVE TO BE?

It depends on who we spend time with. We follow the rules we want to follow, the standard we want to live up to.

I think about my badness this way—if someone followed me around for a week with their phone and recorded everything I said or did, every word, every action, every website visited, how would I feel? Not only that but I was hooked up to a machine that read my mind and displayed my every thought. Then everything was placed online at the end of the week, for all to see, comments open.

I can say right now I would not be comfortable with that. And I'm supposed to be a professional good person. By the way, Christians don't necessarily have better character than others, but a true Christian mourns their badness and strives to be a better person.

Most of us aren't FBI informants, but we are very much imperfect people, with a whole lot of badness in us. If we're honest, we are not as good as we like to think we are.

There are also those who think they are good, or righteous, or moral because of their own ef-

WE ARE NOT AS GOOD AS WE LIKE TO THINK WE ARE.

forts- like they have arrived. Some Christians particularly, carry around a sanctimonious, self-righteous, and elitist attitude, and just like the tax collector in Luke 9:9-14, look down their noses at the rest of us. They are proud of how good they are and think the rest of us are heathen brutes in need of rehabilitation and redemption.

That's not good character, that's terrible.

In fact, that might be even worse than being a bad guy.

If we compare ourselves to what we think are bad guys, we will always look like saints. We are playing to the lowest level of performance, the lowest common denominator.

Ironically, we may also tend to think we look like saints compared to our neighbors.

"I can't believe they are okay with their house looking like that."

"Can they afford that car? Where do they get their money?"

"I would *never* let my kids get away with that."

This is not only judgmental, but also straw-man morality. Who's the best neighbor? Is it really us? We should measure ourselves against a higher, more exemplary standard. I would call this God's standard, and in that case, it's clear—we aren't *even close* to as good as we think we are. In fact, we are all in need of rehabilitation and redemption. The same stuff we think everyone else needs is what we need as well. We all have rotten, decaying junk inside the arteries of our souls in the form of selfishness, comparison, and wishing evil upon others. This garbage clogs up our hearts and prevents us from loving others. It leads to death.

But God is in the business of rehabilitation and redemption. God is in the business of cleaning out the garbage and giving life.

Consider the story of Jesus and Zaccheus, the tax collector in Luke 19:1-10. Jesus is entering Jerusalem. The dusty street is choked with people. Goats are bleating, children are running all around, people are shouting and pushing. They all want to see Jesus better. Some need healing from a disease, some need hope things are going to get better, many are simply curious. Jesus continues into the city. But then, He stops and looks up.

(Huh? Why has he stopped?
What is he looking at?)

The crowd follows Jesus' gaze and looks upward in the same direction. Then they see it.

A grown man has climbed a tree, not fitting with decorum in that time and culture. But there he was, clinging precariously to that gnarled tree limb and watching Jesus pass underneath. Jesus stops, acknowledges the man, and asks to come to his home for dinner.

This seems okay, but the problem is this guy isn't a regular guy. He is Zaccheus, and he is a real bad guy. He was a tax collector for the Romans, the occupying military force in Israel. The Romans were foreigners who didn't speak the local language. For this reason, they liked to use the locals to collect their taxes. Zaccheus knew everyone and what their occupations were. He knew who had cash, who didn't and how much extra people could pay if they had to. Tax collectors often extorted money from the people. The Romans dictated an amount required, and anything raised over that amount was the tax collector's profit. This made Zaccheus, and all tax collectors, coluders with the enemy, traitors, and thieves. Objects of wrath.

But something was going on in Zaccheus. Something inside him wanted to see Jesus for some reason. That something compelled him to break with propriety and climb a tree, since he was short, in order to see Jesus. God was working in Zaccheus' heart, drawing him to Himself, giving him a feeling of mourning for what he had done, and a desire to make it right. He wanted to be better.

NO ONE IS TOO FAR FROM GOD'S LOVE AND FORGIVENESS.

Certainly, by the peoples' standards, Zaccheus was a bad guy. And now Jesus was going to eat and relax and legitimize his house with His presence? The religious elite were stunned, completely incensed as they looked with scorn at Jesus and His new friend, Zaccheus the sinner.

But wait, there's more. While Zaccheus and Jesus walked to his home, God kept working in his life. Perceiving the significance of what Jesus had done and how he had been accepted by Him, Zaccheus repented and confessed his sin. He vowed to give back what he had stolen.

If I have defrauded anyone of anything,

I will give back four times as much.
LUKE 19:8

The "if" clause here strongly suggests that he had defrauded people. Notice he is also giving back, a popular phrase in our culture today. Through this life-altering decision, Zaccheus honored God and Jesus pronounced,

"Salvation has come to this house, because he, too, is a son of Abraham."

Translation: Even though you are a bad guy, you can change.

No one is too far from God's love and forgiveness. We can all change.

We have both good and bad in us. None of us is perfect. The bad in us needs to be healed, removed and forgiven so we can be whole again. Only God can do this. He never gives up on us. Zacheus was bothered by his lack of character. He knew character, or goodness, was found in an authority greater than himself, a just and righteous and kind authority with the ability to proclaim bad people good and give second chances. Like Zaccheus, all we need to do is admit our faults and wrongs to this Authority. God sees the best in us and invites us to become better people.

People with character.

And like Zaccheus, it starts with getting to a place where we can see Him better.

CHAPTER FIVE
RAID

The heavy, clunky walkie-talkies crackled and cackled. Agents affirmed whereabouts and readiness. Everyone was in place. Equipment was secured. A silent prayer uttered. Then, an eerie pause. Hearts pounding so hard they seemed audible. Nerve-racking anticipation.

A quiet peaceful morning about to explode.

Through informants, the FBI learned a lucrative, mob-run Barbut dice (gambling) game was being run from the second story of a home in Cleveland's Little Italy. A raid was planned. Nowadays, this is called executing a search warrant, but in the gritty Mafia days, organized crime agents simply called them raids. From a weaselly, shifty-eyed informant, the investigators learned the entry door to the room upstairs was reinforced with sheet metal, so they determined the plywood-covered windows would be the better place to make initial entrance.

Of course, that sounds so much better.

To get to the second-story window, SWAT agents climbed up on the roof and prepared to rappel down and kick the window open. Everyone nervously awaited the command to execute. Then the moment arrived.

Glass and plywood from the window exploded into the seedy room sending razor-sharp shards of wood and glass onto the table where the residents were seated. Agents hammered away at the door with a sledgehammer. The stunned mobsters looked at the door, then the window, then back at the door.

"FBI! Open up now!"

Bam!...FBI!...Bam!...Bam!

A few seconds later, the entry door and the frame, along with part of the wall imploded into the room leaving a smokey, gaping hole as agents poured through the breach like insects. Drywall dust was suspended in the air, making it hard to see and breathe. Navy blue FBI windbreakers were everywhere.

The mobsters were terrified. They had just been busted by Squad 2 of the Cleveland FBI, and John Sommer was the first agent through the door.

He carried his 12-gauge shotgun loaded with 00 buckshot along with his trusty .357 Magnum revolver on his hip. Don't forget the dark jeans and chunky, bright-white dad shoes, standard issue for white, middle-aged FBI agents in the '80s. No Velcro, no tactical gear, no helmet, kneepads or goggles. Well, not exactly *no* gear. He was wearing a speedloader: a small leather pouch with 6 bullets, seperated into 3 compartments of 2 bullets each. Firearms instructors trained agents to grab 2 bullets at a time for extra reloading speed. Yup, that's when you were really cookin'.

Dad always volunteered for that position, and my mom hated it.

"Let someone without kids do that," she'd say.

It was an argument they regularly had. Dad said after agents had gone through the tough guy stage, nobody really wanted, nor felt the need to be the first one through the door. That's why he volunteered. Someone needed to do it. For him, it was a way to help out the team and serve others.

That's pretty good character.

The agents pointed their revolvers and shotguns. There was only tunnel vision now as the dad-shoes squeaked like a basketball game around the room. They moved quickly and shouted commands, chairs scraped backward from the table on the dull, century-old hardwood floor. Curses filled the air- not a place for little pitchers. The gamblers were told to stand. One dude seemed to pause for a minute before he obeyed, eyes darting back and forth in his skull- as if he was thinking about doing something other than what he was told to do. An experienced agent read the body language, moved swiftly around the corner of the table and pointed a shotgun at the man's head. He got right up.

There was more radio cackle as handcuffs ratcheted tight. Slowly the anxiety died down. The most dangerous moments were over. Voices began to return to normal volumes. The men were frisked as they stood, resembling little boys just sent to the principal's office. A few were armed with cheap, small caliber pistols known as Saturday Night Specials. One had a blackjack—a leather strap with a lead ball at the end, handy for whacking someone into submission. One had a knife. They were all disarmed without incident.

Now the agents could take a breather. Not exactly wearing a Hawaiian shirt sipping a Corona, but moving in that direction. Stress released. A few chuckles. A safe entry, and now everybody in handcuffs. Peace and calm. Whew.

But at the same time you could be more cognizant of what was happening outside your immediate surroundings, the point when you were able identify a smell, a foul stench began to permeate the room.

What is that? It was familiar.

Ah man.

One dejected mobster, the one reticent to stand, began to look more dejected and embarrassed as he steadily fixed his eyes on the floor. Because of the sudden shock and terror of the raid, this guy also experienced anxiety and tunnel vision. And because of that anxiety and tunnel vision, mother nature had taken over. This guy had an accident. Number two. That's right, a big, bad "wise guy", as the Mafia liked to call themselves, had pooped his pants.

Apparently, this sort of thing can happen in high-stress situations, A Navy doctor friend attested that the stress of combat can cause unauthorized bowel movements. To remedy this, soldiers would take a "battle s***t" before going into action.

"You," my dad said, following his nose,

"Sit back down."

One at a time, each man was led out of the room and

ushered downstairs by feds in windbreakers. Only the sitting one was left, guarded by my dad with the shotgun.

My dad looked at the Mafia pooper-trooper and their eyes met.

"Go and clean yourself up," he said.

The large man got up and walked into the dirty antiquated bathroom at the back of the room and closed the door. A few minutes later, he reemerged with a sense of renewed confidence, like a weight had been removed from his chest.

"YOU, SIT BACK DOWN."

"Appreciate it," he said briefly, catching my dad's glance before assuming his regular position of staring back at the floor.

Kindness. Generosity.

These character traits are not required for life. They are extras. Those who have them, we call nice people. During the anxiety of the raid, my dad was able to extend a bit of kindness and generosity to a stranger. When he became a Christian, dad told me he looked for opportunities to minister to the people he encountered. He visited people in prison and he prayed for them. During the Angelo Lonardo protection detail, Dad would often pull out his big leather Bible and practice reading to pass the time. Once Lonardo saw him reading and asked him about it. Dad asked if he wanted to pray together.

"Do you pray, Angelo?" he asked.

"Yeah, I tell 'em I didn't do it!" The man joked.

There are certainly people who don't deserve our kindness and generosity. But instead of giving people what they deserve, God is our moral standard, not what other people think or do. Following God makes us better people.

Love your enemies. Do good to them.
Lend to them without expecting to be repaid.
Then your reward from heaven will be very great,
and you will truly be acting as children of the

Most High, for He Himself is kind
to ungrateful and wicked men.
LUKE 6:35

These radical words by Jesus are just as radical and un-palatable to us today. They are counter-intuitive. They don't make any sense. It's difficult sometimes to be generous or kind, period, let alone to people we dislike or dislike us.

For example, think of the polarization we see in politics today. Many people are in profound and fervent disagree-ment. But don't miss this: God didn't say we needed to like everybody. We don't need to agree with everyone. We don't need to hang out with people who discourage or bring out the worst in us. But we should treat them with kindness.

That means being generous and thoughtful when we are able. And look how Jesus models this later in the book of Luke. This is how He treats His enemies, those who came to arrest and execute Him.

When the other disciples saw what was about to happen,
they exclaimed, 'Lord, should we fight? We brought the
swords!' And one of them struck at the high priest's slave,
slashing off his right ear. But Jesus said, 'No more of this.'
And He touched the man's ear and healed him.
LUKE 22:39-55

Incredible. Even in the midst of his own impending tor-ture and death, Jesus is healing and restoring.

Sometimes we can manage to treat our enemies well, with undeserved kindness and respect. But most of the time it's a choice made outside our feelings, and when we are op-erating outside our feelings, we've entered the realm of disci-pline. We do this because people are special. People are like God.

"Do to others as you would like them to do to you," Jesus says in Luke 6:31.

This might be all we need to sum up the whole idea of character, the whole idea of the Old Testament prophets and the law of Moses, the Ten Commandments, the Golden Rule. It's how we really want to be at the end of the day.

SO MUCH OF CHARACTER IS ABOUT HOW WE TREAT OTHERS.

So much of character is about how we treat others. It's like a litmus test. How is our character? Well, it's really easy. How do we treat other people? In fact, let me offer this, how we treat those we *dislike* reflects our true character.

The next time we are tempted to insult, punish, or curse someone who disagrees with us politically or religiously, is out for our job, bullying our child at school, or lying about us, remember God is kind to people who don't deserve it. He was kind by sending His Son to earth, even though He knew what would happen. He was kind.

For He Himself is kind to wicked and ungrateful men.
LUKE 6:35B

Take a deep breath and take stock of the situation you are in. You may not like the person, and you may not agree with their opinions. That's okay. But you can still be generous and kind, if you want to be.

HOW WE TREAT THOSE WE DISLIKE REFLECTS OUR TRUE CHARACTER.

Is there some way you can take the high ground and show them kindness- instead of giving them what they deserve?

How can you treat them like Jesus?- the way you'd like to be treated?

Then be the first through the door.

CHAPTER SIX
MAFIA MEETING

The old Italian man stopped talking. Not a great sign. My father and his partner paid a visit to a known Mafia associate in Cleveland to get some information. They already had enough to personally charge the man, but he was a little fish. They wanted to learn more about powerful mobsters in his network and hoped he might give up names, accidentally or intentionally, from the pressure of the interrogation. The organized crime agents constantly conducted interviews like this, hoping to worry wise guys into turning on each other. Using little fish to get the big fish.

His petite and friendly wife who spoke minimal English invited the agents in, welcoming them as if were long-lost relatives. She offered the agents wine as she led them to the back patio of the home. They declined.

Before them was the man they came to talk to. He was not a high-up guy in the organization, not what the Mafia called a "made man," who was an official member. But he aspired to be and was willing to show what he could do. Associates were sort of like the errand boys, the ones who brought the made men their coffee, emptied the trash, did the grunt work. It was unusual this man was older, but not a made member. He began his career of choice a bit later, or perhaps this was a retirement gig.

He didn't look all that intimidating or malevolent, either, dressed in a casual collared shirt, slacks with black socks, slippers. Behind him, drying cloves of garlic hung on rows of twine, eagerly awaiting to be added to the next batch of sauce.

The conversation with the man began cordially

enough. Niceties, Cleveland Browns frustrations, complaints about the weather, normal Clevelander conversation. Then John Sommer shifted gears and pulled out a big yellow legal pad and began asking questions. As the questions drew closer to the man's criminal activity, his countenance began to sour, and a scowl grew on his chubby, wrinkled face. Finally, he stopped talking, folded his arms across his great beer belly, and stared at the agents with a frown.

"Uh, could you answer the question, sir?" asked my dad.

"I'm waiting," replied the Mafia hopeful.

"For what?"

"For you to show me some respect," he said, in a gravelly, hoarse voice.

My dad and his partner exchanged puzzled glances.

After an explanation with a raised voice, the now-animated mobster revealed he was offended with the questions my father asked. He considered his finances personal and felt the agents were being rude by asking about his income. That was only for family and friends. The agents weren't friends.

As ridiculous as this line of reasoning was, something rang home with me when I was told about this encounter. The man wanted to be respected. Even if he didn't deserve respect, which you could certainly make a case that he didn't, he wanted it. In fact, he was so driven in his desire to be respected that he sought it from the most unlikely of sources. His enemies.

The conversation turned strained as the agents continued. The visit wasn't going well anymore. Awkward, pregnant pauses. More raised voices and anger. After a few more minutes, the agents got up to leave. Cursing in Italian and flipping them off, the irascible man followed them back into the house towards the door. His wife opened it for them with a smile. Now the agents were ticked off.

Getting flipped off can bring out a primitive part in us.

Standing at the car, my dad and his partner exchanged incensed glances and stood there for a bit, cooling their tempers. We're done for today. There would be another time to interview this guy.

Respect is important to us. Just as some signal their virtue for all to see, others transmit their respectability. Our job titles, the model and make of car we drive, where we go for spring break, the brand of clothes we wear and the neighborhood we live in are all respectability indicators, telling others just where we stand in the pecking order and how much respect we are due.

My kids are concerned about having newer phones because they look at each other's phones. That is a signal of social standing and respectability. One of the first things we still ask each other when we meet is what we do. That, along with where we live, defines us initially to others. In our heads, we ask ourselves what we think about someone's answers, and make value judgments about their respectability. Of course within every profession, there are indicators of who deserves the most respect in the organization.

Make no mistake, the professional Christian world is just as enamored with respect.

Pastors and ministers compare themselves to other pastors, almost always by church or ministry attendance. Numbers are how we feel good about our ministry- whether we consider it, and ourselves, successful or not. This is totally normal, understandable and reasonable. It's just not God's way. He doesn't determine success the same way we do. Understand, numbers are not bad. They represent people. But numbers can corrupt if our motives are not pure.

After numbers, we compare by how often one receives speaking invitations at notable retreats and conferences, and whether we have a podcast or not, and how many subscribers, and whether we've written books and how many, and how many copies sold- by the way, this book is not gonna give me a ton of gravitas in the professional Christian world. I'm spilling too many secrets here!

Spiritual leaders compare and compare to see where we stand in respectability in relation to one another. Often, this comparison means competition.

Years ago I was the director of a ministry on a large university. I wanted to see our group grow and reach people on campus for Christ. That meant I wanted our group to be the biggest and the best. So when another ministry began encroaching on what I thought was our territory, I became competitive. I sincerely wanted the other ministry to fail and ours to be the dominant Christian influence on campus.

GOD DOESN'T WANT SOMEONE WHO CAN SCORE TOUCHDOWNS IN MINISTRY.

Nice Christian attitude, huh?

So here's one thing I've learned through periods of incredible stripping and refining in twenty-six years of professional ministry: God doesn't want someone who can score touchdowns in ministry- we do. God doesn't need our touchdowns. He's more interested in our hearts.

The Mafia guy was also right. As a fellow human being, he did deserve respect. It didn't matter if he was evil or not. This doesn't mean he was entitled to not answer the questions, but he was permitted genuine respect and honor. And giving this respect and honor is a part of having good character. All people are worthy of dignity simply because we are people.

The Bible speaks to our innate self-worth through the creation story.

Then God said, 'Let Us make people in Our image, after Our likeness, to rule over the fish of the sea and the birds of the air, over the livestock, and over all the earth itself and every creature that crawls upon it.' So God created people in His own image; in the image of God He created him; male and female He created them.
GENESIS 1:26-27

Every human being that has ever lived is made in the image of God. Notice, we are not God but are made in His likeness. This is so neat because it means we look like God, we sound like God, we act like God. Think about that for a minute. Humans bear a similarity to God. Our children resemble us because they are created from our DNA, and we resemble our parents. People say things like,

"You look like your mother."

"I can see your father in you."

"Ha! You sound just like your sister."

"Stop acting like your brother!"

Our kids get our chin, nose, mannerisms, our good and bad qualities.

We can see a glimpse of God in each one of His creations.

At the same time, we also shouldn't insist on respect. Often in life, we will not receive it, and we need to decide how we will deal with that frustration. When the time comes, we will either demand our rights, let someone have it publicly on Twitter, or denigrate their reputation behind their back.

Or we will extend forgiveness and patience. Instead of insisting on being right, we could be patient. Maybe we don't react or fight back if it's not that big of a deal. Not everything is a moral imperative. Respond, but don't react.

The word "triggered" is popular today. I've seen a few articles with trigger warnings at the beginning. On one hand, this is good because it means we are gaining emotional awareness of ourselves, acknowledging and validating what's going on inside of us. That is a good thing. But it's also implied that one should not be triggered, nor should we trigger someone else because being triggered is bad. That sounds okay, but at the same time, it's not a realistic or healthy view of life. It's not possible to go through life without being triggered. We are human beings, praise God, and we will all be triggered by certain things- as we should. And we cannot shield ourselves from everything that is upsetting or discouraging. That wouldn't build resilience, a very necessary skill for survival and thriving in life. Life is hard and we are emotional beings. I once had a roommate whose goal was to be like a character on Star Trek named Data. Apparently, Data is known for not having, or at least not making, any decision based upon emotion.

All I'll say is I don't recall my roommate being successful in any romantic relationship.

But nor is it healthy to be so emotionally on edge that a small slight or careless word, or someone disagreeing with us on social media will cause us to fire. Thick skin and a soft heart is a good way to go through life.

We can give up our right to receive respect while giving respect to others. This is precisely what Jesus did when He allowed Himself to die on the cross.

Have this attitude in yourselves which was also in Christ Jesus, who, although He existed in the form of God, did not regard equality with God a thing to be grasped, but emptied Himself, taking the form of a servant, and being made in the likeness of men. Being found in appearance as a man, He humbled Himself by becoming obedient to the point of death, even death on a cross.
PHILIPPIANS 2:5-8

Jesus, the One most worthy of respect, voluntarily gave up His right to having respect from us, His very creation. He allowed Himself to be publicly humiliated and shamed; dying naked on a cross for all to see. No dignity, no mercy.

Incidentally, this is what we require of the difficult job of law enforcement today. Those with a badge and gun ingest toxic levels of evil every day. The fact that we expect these men and women to not react in kind proves we know what right and wrong are.

Our human nature compels us to criticize and slander each other because we want to be at the top of the pecking order. The Bible uses colorful words, *"bite and devour one another"* in Galatians 5:15. We do this because we demand our rights. We want to win, and we want other people to lose. It might sound ugly to say that out loud, but deep inside, we know it's true.

At the same time, many of us desire to possess good character deep in our souls. We really do want to be good people, and that desire for goodness is from our creator. We should act on that desire. When we do, we are acting like God.

WE WANT TO WIN, AND WE WANT OTHER PEOPLE TO LOSE.

Every person is worthy of dignity and respect whether we agree with them or not, whether they are vaccinated or not, whether they voted for Trump, support Black Lives Matter, have a different faith than us, are gay, straight, transgender, speak a different language, or have a different skin color.

The person of character understands this and knows the mark of good character can be measured by how we react when we are treated unfairly or disrespectfully. Adversity has a way of squeezing out whatever is inside us.

Will we respond with kindness and respect, or will we repay evil for evil?

CHAPTER SEVEN
SHOOTOUT

April 11, 1986. The Miami shootout. The FBI's most tragic day.

One normal, chilly spring day in the mid-1980s', my mom picked me up from middle school and gave me a ride home. As I got into the car, she told me right away something awful had happened. There had been a terrible shootout in Miami, Florida. FBI agents had been killed. All I heard was the "agents killed" part, and instantly a wave of panic crashed over me. My stomach dropped and I felt nauseous. Then she said my dad was okay.

Instant relief.

Michael Platt and William Matix were former Army Rangers. They had served together and were close friends. Through a series of emotional problems, failed marriages and business ventures, the militarized pair turned to making a living through armed robbery. Matix was even a suspect in his own wife's disappearance and subsequent murder years prior. They terrorized suburban Miami for months, killing anyone who got in their way as they robbed banks and armored cars. Finally, the FBI tracked and identified the killers through constant stakeouts in a Miami suburb. Once again, anxiety, uncertainty, and tension were undoubtedly the primary emotions of the agents involved. A survivor of the gunfight substantiated this afterward when he told his ghastly story.

Incidentally, if you're catching that a recurring theme for FBI agents, at least in those days, was anxiety, John Sommer would say that was correct. Of course, there is also anxiety today, but it seems to come less frequently than years ago. Maybe that is because of the overall decline in organized crime. I know many retired agents who had several close calls during their careers. Thankfully, it seems like there are fewer close calls today. Agents tell me most of their stress comes from executing search warrants. Anything can happen on a search warrant, and most of what can happen is bad. An agent never know what awaits them when they are the first through the door. There is always a risk.

With moments of sheer terror anticipating life or death confrontations, it makes you wonder why people sign up for the job. For many, I suspect it has to do with aspiring to the character of the mission. Fidelity, bravery, and integrity. It has to do with protecting people and bringing about justice. A young agent told me he turned down several employment opportunities with better pay because he wanted something that felt like he was making a difference. That's why my dad did it. In fact, the job was so compelling to him that he often said he would do it for free.

But for agents with families, it was not just the agent who signed up for the job. It was a cost borne by everyone. It cost our family, and it cost others more. One night, a drug squad agent was sleeping soundly in his bed when he was startled awake to the heartbeat-skipping sound of shattering glass downstairs. Flying down with a gun in his hand and bedroom slippers on his feet, he found a brick had been thrown through his front window. Crudely scrawled on it were the words, "Your kids are dead". The family was forced to receive twenty-four-hour protection for several months until they found a new home.

BEING WILLING TO PAY A COST DOESN'T TAKE AWAY THE FEAR.

For other families, the cost is still even greater.

Being willing to pay a cost doesn't take away the fear, though.

Eight agents in five cars trailed the suspects for several

miles along a busy suburban street, praying to follow the car to a less-crowded area before pulling it over. But when four regular-looking sedans, each with two clean-cut white guys in the front seats made the exact turn as the suspect's car, they caught on. The element of surprise was gone. The fugitives knew they were being followed.

Desperate to apprehend the killers now, the agents attempted to run them off the road. One car drove in front of the suspect's car to cut it off and two others agonizingly scraped in along the sides. Now the car was boxed in. Burnt rubber filled the air as the long, heavy sedans screeched, banged, and crashed into each other. One of the suspects giggled, as if he were enjoying a ride at an amusement park.

The car maneuvering battle continued. Finally the suspects' car ran up a curb, plowed into a tree and came to an abrupt, smoking stop.

I'm not sure if any of the agents were wearing leather speedloaders at that time, but it probably wouldn't have made any difference for what came next.

A desperate gunfight began. Michael Platt was heavily armed with a Mini-14 semiautomatic rifle, and William Matix had a 12-gauge shotgun. Each had .357 Magnum revolvers. Platt leapt out of his mangled Monte Carlo and opened fire with deafening blasts from the Mini-14. Glass dust from windows exploded into the air, landing in the hair and on the arms of the agents. They scrambled out of their cars now, in a life-or-death situation, crouching and returning fire with their handguns. It was fight or flight, yet no one on either side was flying. At least, not yet.

One horrific second dragged by after another as the men jockeyed for optimal position, sought cover, and looked for a clear shot. Platt was hit early with a 9mm pistol round and then with a .38 revolver bullet. More hits came, yet he would not end his rampage. He was on a death mission, probably the mission he secretly always wanted. Like a stirred-up hornet's nest, each wound seemed to invigorate him more. With each hit he grew more hateful.

But it wasn't over yet.

Matix was shot in the shoulder and sat incapacitated, in shock in the front seat. Then, a burst of fire from Platt caused window glass to explode into the eyes of Agent Ben Grogan, his glasses flew off his face onto the ground. Unable to see clearly, he stepped backward and crushed the glass lenses. Matix quickly made use of this disadvantage and shot Grogan in the neck, severing his spinal cord and killing him instantly.

Agent Jerry Dove had a terrible feeling. He was pulling the trigger, but his gun wouldn't fire. Frantically, he stopped to study his pistol more closely. It was shot through the center, locking the slide back and rendering it useless. It was then Dove noticed Grogan, lying motionless on the ground, but he didn't see Platt creep around the car and raise his rifle. Dove was shot multiple times at close range, execution-style.

Grogan and Dove were now dead and five other agents lay bleeding in the street, seriously wounded.

But it wasn't over yet.

Michael Platt dragged his tattered body over to an FBI sedan and attempted to start it. William Matix somehow extracted himself from the Monte Carlo and joined Platt. They were trying to escape!

Agent Edmundo Mireles was watching what was happening. He had been hit in his left forearm, shattering the bone and causing it to hang uselessly at his side. Sheltering behind a car, Mireles braced himself against the bumper and fired several shotgun blasts with only his right arm, squeezing the stock with his legs as he racked each shell until he was out of ammo. He dropped the heavy gun.

But it still wasn't over.

Dangerously courting shock and faint from blood loss, Mireles mustered his bravery, all his remaining strength, and drew his service revolver. He stood up and charged the suspect's bullet-riddled car, firing until the gun clicked empty and finally killed them both.

When Platt succumbed to his wounds, he had been shot twelve times, receiving two fatal wounds as he continued to fight. Medical professionals said he ran on pure adrenaline and evil willpower, though mortally wounded.

Now, I was worried about the safety of my dad. Before that time, I never experienced much anxiety about the risks that went with my dad's job. But after the Miami shootings, things changed. I felt an unsettling from that day forward until the end of his career. Having an FBI agent dad was cool, but it became less cool if he might be killed in a gun battle one day while you're at school. I was grateful Dad came home that night. Not all moms and dads do come back. Every day after that, I worried a little bit until he walked through the door.

Jerry Dove and Ben Grogan, the two agents who were killed, were household names in my home. We all knew them. Years later, a movie called *In the Line of Fire: The FBI Shootings*[5] came out. Watching that movie today over twenty-five years later still gives me that same pit-in-my-stomach feeling when I was a little kid.

Most law enforcement personnel are people of principle. That is, they feel compelled or driven to do the job for a greater cause, usually for the good and protection of others. They know there is always a chance they won't make it home, yet they accept those risks. There's selflessness there, a willingness to give up one's well-being for the sake of others.

That morning, the agents got up, went to work, and went about their day. Just like any other day.

It just happened to be a really bad day.

A day that called for true courage, and strength of character.

When they spotted the armed and dangerous suspects in their car, no agent asked to be let out at the nearest 7-Eleven. None of them drove away. When the shootout began and the agents realized they were sorely outgunned, no one dropped their handgun and ran for cover, although the instinct of self-preservation was likely bellowing to do so. I'm sure they fought that instinct every moment.

No, they stayed, and it cost many of them their emotional and physical well-being. They were injured, traumatized, scarred, and wounded for life. For a few, it cost their lives.

That's admirable character.

Putting others before ourselves is part of the essence of character. It's an axiom of the Christian story. It's about sacrifice.

> *For this is how God loved the world: He gave His one and only Son, so that everyone who believes in Him will not perish but have eternal life.*
> JOHN 3:16

There's an exchange happening here. Jesus' life for ours. He dies and we live- because He loved us. There is a price to be paid for the evil and brokenness in us, and Jesus volunteered to be the One to accept the cost and pay for it. He claimed to be the Creator of the earth, the Son of God, the Ruler of the universe. Yet He left Heaven to take the form of a helpless baby, born in an unsanitary, smelly living space for animals and placed in their food bowl.

Yes, their food bowl.

Then after receiving almost no education, He worked a blue-collar job until He was thirty-three years old. No college degree, no car, no house of His own, no family. He became a public mockery and was unjustly executed by men who spat in His face as they cursed Him. The Bible tells us He did this for one reason: Not because it felt good, not because He was trying to prove a point (Exactly what point would that be?), but because He wanted to make a way for us to know Him. Jesus died to pay the penalty for our sins. The penalty we rightly owed. Why?

COURAGE MEANS WE STAND. SACRIFICE MEANS WE STAND FIRM.

Because that's justice. That's what justice demands. But then He paid the penalty Himself. Why? Because of His grace and mercy.

God loved us and loves us.

Courage and sacrifice are two stalwarts of character. Courage means we stand. Sacrifice means we stand firm. Not because it's safe, not because it's expedient to do so, but because it's the right thing to do. When the shootouts of our lives come, we want to be the kind of person who doesn't drive away but stands firm and fights.

That's who we want to be on the inside. It takes character to get it done.

CHAPTER EIGHT
UNDERCOVER

My dad worked organized crime and sometimes that meant undercover. There was a squad of full-time undercover or surveillance agents who did most of the work, but other agents did a stint in these duties if it was necessary for cases like our good friends from the Mafia.

The mob ran rampant in Cleveland in the '70s and '80s. In those decades, local businesses and labor unions were terrorized, extorted, and robbed- in any order. Tractor-trailers were stolen. People went missing. Mob associates or wise guys were found shot to death and shoved in the trunks of cars. None of this macabre underworld was visible to the casual observer or work commuter- until it spilled out onto the streets. It finally did. In 1976, 36 car bombs were detonated in Mafia-connected murders. Newspapers began calling Cleveland "Bomb City, U.S.A."

The FBI worked around the clock to take down these vicious organizations, and one of their strategies was to provide investment opportunities for the bad guys, in the form of undercover agents. Like a fisherman uses a lure to fool a fish (more fishing analogies), the Bureau enticed the Mafia with succulent, flashy and naïve new investors.

My dad was one of those phony investors. I never saw him dressed like this. Those were the "Bye can't tell you where I'm going" nights. But he described his ridiculous undercover costume as a mustache- he could grow one in just a few days, hair slicked back, black turtleneck with a long gold chain over top (Dad never wore a chain in his life), several gold rings (and only his wedding ring), wool slacks with, wait for it: high-heeled zip-up disco boots. (I so wish I could've seen this. I checked his closet several times for them.) Legit fake drivers' license with a fake name. You must also act the part. Add in a potty mouth and obnoxiously flash cash everywhere. Lean, mean, and ready to party. Perfect.

If you would've known my dad prior, you would have been genuinely stunned to learn they were the same person.

During a meeting with newly minted mob members called soldiers and the paper-shredding associates in a deserted parking garage, one of the full-time undercover agents wore a wire while completing a drug deal, secretly recording everything. This was the mid-80's and let's just say the technology wasn't where it is today. Wearing a wire meant lugging around a big, fat tape recorder under your clothes. Not digital, but analog, mind you, and a cassette tape that made a mechanical click sound when it started or stopped. You had to stuff the recorder in your waistband. But this time, the wise guys got wiser and frisked the agent before the drug deal was transacted, just to make sure he wasn't a fed. The criminal's hands felt the agent's arms, then down to the sides, to the waist, and then stopped on the recorder. Time stood still. The agent held his breath. A lifetime came down to the next few seconds.

"That your gun?" asked the Mafia soldier. Because bad guys carry guns.

"Yup," said the agent.

The bad guy bought it, and the agent lived to tell me the story.

Another chief hallmark of character is congruency. That is, simply not being a hypocrite.

We all know what a hypocrite is—they say one thing but do another. To have good character, you must follow through with what you say you will do. You can't delete the tweets and say you got hacked. Character means you don't act one way in front of one person, then turn around and say the opposite to another, or throw someone under the bus to gain favor. Or lie.

That's not good character- in any culture or time in history.

Abraham from the Old Testament lied. Yes, he was also the father of the Jewish people. Not on one, but two occasions, he lied at the border to the Egyptian customs agent about his wife not being his wife. Their family was trying to move to a more fertile region for farming and livestock and Abraham lied because the host country would take what they wanted in exchange for immigration. Because Sarah was beautiful, Abraham feared they would take his wife Sarah for the king and kill him. So, Abraham lied. Instead of trusting God, Abraham chose to make his own way forward and trafficked his wife. Thankfully, God intervened to save the situation and gave Abraham his wife back. But he did the exact same thing later in his life.

Then Isaac his son, who also had a beautiful wife, followed in his father's footsteps and lied about his relationship with Rebecca when entering a foreign country. Like father, like son. Often, we do what is expedient to survive, not what is right.

GOSSIP IS INCONGRUENCY OF CHARACTER.

Gossip is an incongruency of character. I'll define gossip as negative talk about someone else that makes them appear foolish or incompetent. It may be false or it may be true, but it doesn't need to be said. Gossip is trash-talking. When you say these things, you are building an alliance between you and the other person against the one being talked about. This can be exhilarating, talking about some illicit fact or secret. That's why it's appealing. But when the person walks in the room, we pretend like everything's great. This two-faced behavior is incongruent and deceptive to the other person. It's a form of lying and having a laugh at the expense of someone else. No one wants people talking behind their back. When I've done this myself, I've justified it, telling myself they deserve it or I'm "helping" them somehow by bringing it into the light.

As my kids would say: nah bruh. That's still wrong.

It's not my responsibility to change people.

We can partake in gossip by listening, even if we're not doing the talking. Listening enables the gossiper to do their destructive work. It gives them an audience.

Complaining can become gossip because it often makes the one complained against appear inept or stupid. Complaining is very understandable, universal, and everyone complains at times, but that doesn't make it a good thing. Once again, the Bible guides us clearly:

> *Do all things without complaining or arguing.*
> PHILIPPIANS 2:14

Expressing reasonable concern or frustration is different than complaining. And complaining is different than venting or getting something off our chest. Sometimes we need to release anger or tension verbally to a safe or empathetic listener.

I've also become more cognizant of when I may be gossiping, supporting gossip by listening, or complaining. Then I have the choice to continue or not. I ask God for the strength to cut off the interaction and excuse myself.

It is, however, my responsibility to shape and mold and change my kids. I wouldn't be a good father if I didn't intervene. For adults, I wait for an invitation to speak into someone's life.

There are more biblical examples of lying, deception, and gossip. Jacob from the Old Testament was also a liar. His father was dying, and Semitic tradition called for the father the bless the oldest son and bequeath him the wealth and status as the new head of the household. A passing of the baton, so to speak. Esau, Jacob's brother, was the oldest son, so he was in line to become the successor. But Jacob and his mother Rebecca, who favored Jacob, wanted Jacob to be given the official birthright. It probably started with gossip, complaining about the things they didn't like about Esau, but then the gossip turned to action and led to Jacob and Rebecca cooking up (pun intended) a scheme to trick his father. Jacob masqueraded as Esau to his blind, demented father, as he brought him his favorite meal. The plan worked and Isaac unknowingly gave Jacob the blessing and title of the firstborn.

The Israelites complained and trash-talked Moses behind his back. David's men gossiped about him. Sennacherib, the king of Assyria, heard a rumor, likely some gossip, and turned his whole army around from besieging Jerusalem. Gossip, lying, and triangulation led to the death of Jesus.

I remember my mom explaining to me how trusted John Sommer was by the Bureau. The FBI frequently asked him to count the massive amounts of cash, diamonds, and jewelry confiscated during organized crime raids. There was always a lot of gold jewelry on hand. The case agent dropped everything in my dad's backseat in banker's boxes to be inventoried. As the evidence expert, Dad checked for fingerprints, hairs and fibers, and other clues, and he did so alone. I'm sure this is different today, but back then, no one supervised his work. He just submitted a report and handed back the evidence. My mom explained how he could have easily slipped some of those valuables into his pocket from time to time. Evidence can disappear.

"And we could use extra money," my mom said.

I marveled at the integrity and trustworthiness of my dad, and I was proud.

When FBI agents went undercover with their gold chains and disco boots, the Mafia was ensnared by a lie- just like a fish that falls for a lure. And like the fish, the lie often led to their demise. Undercover agents made the Mafia say things that, had they known the truth, they wouldn't have wanted to say. Reveal things they wouldn't want to have revealed. Trust people they shouldn't have trusted.

The same thing happens to us. We can be taken down by

lies and false beliefs.

> *Stolen bread is sweet, but afterward it*
> *turns to gravel in the mouth.*
> **PROVERBS 20:17**

No one wants to eat gravel. Telling the truth is something most of us learned we should do when we were kids. Lying is wrong and brings negative consequences. It still applies. Telling the truth is good character.

Are you a liar, a gossiper, a complainer? Are you two-faced?

It's OK, we can be honest with ourselves. No one here is judging us. God knows everything already.

If we don't like who we are, we can change.

We change ourselves by changing our character.

CHAPTER NINE
ARREST

John Sommer arrested many people in his career. I don't know the exact number, but once he gave me a clue.

"A lot of people have looked down the barrel of this gun, Scott," he once said matter-of-factly, with a straight face. We were shooting together at the range.

I laughed to myself. I mean, who says that?

But someone else was about to look down that barrel, as well.

"See that car right there? Go get into the back-seat."

In the mid-'80s in Cleveland, my dad stopped in a downtown neighborhood to call into the FBI office. The sky had darkened early, as usual for Cleveland in the Wintertime. He needed to relay some important information in to the organized crime squad. In those days there were no iPhones; the only way to make a call was to find a payphone. A payphone required stopping, getting out of your car, and entering a small, lighted glass booth. You put in a quarter and made a local call. Doing this in certain locations at certain times of the day exposed you- making you an easy target to get mugged.

While my dad stood in the glass booth, he noticed three men sauntering towards the phone in a casual, but deliberate trajectory. They were eying him like a hawk waiting to swoop in for the kill. The men slowly approached. One looked like he held a pad of paper in his hand. Not the big yellow legal pad this time.

Without interrupting the conversation he was having with the switchboard attendant, my dad pulled back his overcoat, and his shiny stainless-steel revolver gleamed in the moonlight.

"Woah, woah, woah!" One of the guys said and backed up with his hands in the air.

"See that car right there? Go get into the backseat," my dad said, pointing to his car, his partner sitting in the passenger seat.

"I knew you were a cop... I knew it!" the man squeaked, as he and his little band scurried back into the darkness from where they had burrowed.

Thinking later about the encounter, I realized the would-be mugger was pretty foolish. Not too wise, actually. Basically, he thought reality was one way, but he was incorrect in his perception. He misjudged my dad. He also failed to see the occupant in the parked car, meaning they weren't alone. Overall, it's fair to say the man lacked wisdom. He didn't think he was trying to mug a federal agent. That was a foolish thing to do, and the guy barely avoided arrest.

The Bible has a lot to say about wisdom.

Wisdom is the principal thing; Therefore, get wisdom.
And in all your getting, get understanding.
PROVERBS 4:7

The fear of the LORD is the beginning of wisdom,
And the knowledge of the Holy One is understanding.
PROVERBS 9:10

If any of you lacks wisdom, you should ask God, who
gives generously to all without finding fault, and it
will be given to you.
JAMES 1:5

Much of wisdom is about exercising good judgment or foresight. Wisdom comes from life experience.

Following experience, wisdom comes from trusted sources—people, books, podcasts, certain places on the internet, the library. Trusted sources are the key. We need to trust where the information is coming from.

The Bible encourages us to seek out those who possess wisdom. As an aside, if you don't have a mentor that can give you wisdom, that would be a great idea. Find someone who is wiser, more experienced, or better in your field or skill, or just life. Hire a life coach- I know a good one if you're interested. If you're a Christian, find someone who's been a Christian longer. Then watch, learn, and ask questions. Be a learner.

WISDOM COMES FROM LIFE EXPERIENCE.

You will need to be deliberate in finding a mentor. Mentors don't usually materialize on their own. You'll need to ask directly, "Will you be my mentor?" and be clear about your expectations or desires.

There is a big difference between wisdom and knowledge. Knowledge is knowing facts. Wisdom is knowing how to use those facts; therefore, life experience greatly increases wisdom.

If someone doesn't have life experience, that person has less wisdom. They might have enormous head knowledge and be the smartest person in the room, but the amount of wisdom they possess is small.

Younger people may have talent or skills, but they have less wisdom. That doesn't mean they're bad, they're just less wise. You gain wisdom as you get older. Experience is our teacher.

This means Christians should look for older, wiser pastors and teachers to learn from.

Young pastors are popular today. They look good and feel good. They may be highly skilled orators or possess strong managerial skills.

SKILL DOES NOT QUALIFY SOMEONE FOR SPIRITUAL LEADERSHIP.

These are appreciable qualities helpful in the execution of ministry, but they can be learned. Skill does not qualify someone for spiritual leadership. What takes a lot more time and effort to cultivate is character- what's going on inside our hearts.

Competency matters, but character matters more.

COMPETENCY MATTERS, BUT CHARACTER MATTERS MORE.

Remember when God sent Samuel to look for the new king of Israel in 1 Samuel 16:5-10? Jesse paraded seven of his sons past Samuel on an Ancient Near East catwalk. The sexiest, most outwardly attractive sons were the ones Samuel was sure the Lord would choose to be king. But God reminded him that people look at the outward appearance, but the Lord looks at the heart.

If you've been following Christ for a while, you know how hard-fought humility, brokenness and integrity are. These character traits only come through the stripping nature of difficult life experiences, when we have come to the end of ourselves. Young spiritual leaders simply have not had enough time to marinate in these spaces. And that's okay. When Paul tells Timothy not to let others make conclusions about him because of his youth (1 Timothy 4:12), it likely meant Timothy was the exception, not the rule.

Education is also important. Learning from people smarter than we are expands our thinking and gets us out of our echo chamber. It helps us understand people better. Formal biblical and seminary training isn't required to be a spiritual leader, but is always positive and increases wisdom.

Look for mentors with significant life experience who can offer time-tested truths smelted and purified by the furnace of real life; not just the good speakers, the enthralling personalities, the attractive exterior.

Most people want to be wise. God has given us the ability to be so through our ability to learn from experience. We exercise that wisdom through discipline.

"See that guy right there? I've probably arrested him 5

times."

One sunny, summer morning in Cleveland, Ohio, my dad and I drove downtown together. The funny thing about Cleveland is, it doesn't matter how high the temperature climbs during the day, it's always freezing cold in the morning near Lake Erie. I was interning with the FBI that summer, and we had taken the scenic route along the lake, passing small businesses along the way. We were stopped at a traffic light and my dad looked over at a small Italian bistro.

And there was the man.

My dad and his partner had entered a sleazy, mobbed-up, Westside Cleveland bar at an opportune time. A known Mafia intern was sitting at the bar laughing and drinking whiskey shots. He was holding a bulging envelope of bills in front of himself on the bar. Then the door creaked open and slammed and two federal agents walked in. Talk about bad timing. The guy took one look at Dad and startled when he recognized him. He began to push the bills across the bar to the bartender, who also noticed the agents. Realizing what was happening, my dad quickened his pace and slammed his hand down on top of the envelope just before it reached its destination.

"I'll take that," my dad said, scooping up the bills and drawing his gun while his partner handcuffed the man.

To my dad, something didn't look right. He had already arrested the man several times. The bad guy claimed to be unemployed, but now had a huge wad of cash? So John Sommer canceled the transaction and both the early-morning-whiskey-drinker and the bartender were arrested. The money became evidence from an illegal gambling outfit.

"Some people never learn," my dad said with a shrug, as we passed the man.

"He does the same thing over and over again."

I heard this from other organized crime agents as well. After their prison sentences were completed, many suspects went right back to their lives of crime. An agent whose dad was also an agent told me he's going after the kids of the people who his dad put in prison. Generational curses.

It was weird to be looking straight at a criminal that my dad knew personally. Also weird, was that he was sitting outside at 7 in the morning at a restaurant that wasn't open. I also had a weird feeling when the dude looked straight at me as we drove by.

Come to think of it, the whole thing was pretty weird.

Some people never learn. I chewed on that for a long time.

I hate admitting this in print, but I can relate. For me, it's not a matter of lacking the knowledge or wisdom, it's a matter of discipline. The bottom line is, I just like to do what I like to do. I like doing what's comfortable and feels good. That's how I feel most of the time. But that is a problem. It's a short-term perspective. Discipline requires a long-term vision because discipline doesn't feel good at the time. I mentored several division one college athletes during my ministry, often attending practices and observing their training up close. For college athletes, their sport is serious business. They train constantly to perfect their bodies and performance. The athletes don't do it because swimming practices at 5:30 in the morning feel good. They do it because they are exercising discipline and have a long-term vision. Some hope to be drafted by a minor league farm team, some are training for the Olympics. They all have goals they are striving for, and that's what drives them to get out of a warm bed each morning to make their feet hit the cold floor.

Sometimes we make the same poor choices repeatedly. We lack discipline. We lack long-term vision. The book of Hebrews addresses this with the story of Moses in the Old Testament.

DISCIPLINE REQUIRES LONG-TERM VISION.

By faith Moses, when he had grown up, refused to be called the son of Pharaoh's daughter, choosing

rather to endure ill-treatment with the people of
God than to enjoy the passing pleasures of sin.
HEBREWS 11:24-25

You can see Moses' long-term vision. Instead of temporarily enjoying the pleasures of Egypt, he chose to identify with the Jewish people instead, the slaves of the land. Read that again, the slaves. If you know the story, Moses was raised in the house of Pharaoh the king of Egypt by his daughter, the princess. Though he was adopted by the princess and a Hebrew by birth, he held the enviable status of royalty. The lofty privileges he enjoyed set him unattainably apart from his own Hebrew people as well as the common Egyptians. Now why in the world would you give that up?

We may not realize this, but ancient Egypt had many of the same luxuries we have today. Delicious food, famously soft linen clothing, warm baths, beautiful jewelry, cool chariots, nice homes, sports and live entertainment were theirs to enjoy. Moses deliberately chose, through a series of events, to leave his life of comfort and luxury and became the leader of the slaves, the outcasts and aliens of the country.

Eventually, God punished Pharaoh by destroying Egypt and Moses led the Israelite people out of Egypt into the promised land. There, they formed their own country, the nation of Israel. But not before they learned a valuable lesson about discipline.

NO ONE GETS MARRIED PLANNING TO GET A DIVORCE.

It took serious discipline and powerful long-term perspective for Moses to give up his cushy, luxurious life. But God has given us the ability to discipline ourselves.

For God has not given us a spirit of timidity
but of power, love, and discipline.
2 TIMOTHY 1:7

No discipline seems pleasant at the time, but painful.
Later, however, it produces a harvest of righteousness
and peace for those who have been trained by it.
HEBREWS 12:11

As a final aside, if you are a Christian or church-goer, you may have heard the term discipline used before in a sermon or Bible study.

The *spiritual disciplines* are practices a Christian does because of their faith. They include activities like prayer and meditation, reading the Bible, memorizing scripture, fasting, worship, attending church, giving financially, and serving others. Doing these things doesn't get us into Heaven. We do them not to earn God's favor, but because we already have it. They are ways we can thank God for what He's done for us and grow in our connection with Him. They also help develop our character. An excellent book to learn more about the spiritual disciplines and how to incorporate them into your life is *The Spiritual Disciplines Handbook* by Adele Ahlberg Calhoun.[6]

Church discipline refers to a local church applying punishment to a member because of their actions.

This is an important subject, so before we address it, we should take a brief moment and define a few principles used to study the Bible.

Exegesis, or lifting the meaning out of scripture, is discovering an author's original, intended meaning for the original, intended audience. Sound exegesis requires the discipline of only interpreting what the text says, leaving behind as much as possible of our personal bias and present-day context. All we're looking for is what was written and translated.

There are occasionally times when literary devices are employed such as metaphors, or prophetic and apocalyptic text might have dual meanings. These are often clearly noted in a good study Bible.

Application is the next step. The Bible was written thousands of years ago. In light of that, what does God want us to know or do as modern readers today?

We should first consider how the original audience likely understood and applied the text. Trusted commentaries from historians and scholars can be helpful here. There's a distinction needed between continuities and discontinuities. Not everything applicable in the Ancient Near East is applicable to us today as moderns. Some things do not transcend the time/culture gap. For example, cultural practices regarding food, dress, tattoos, hairstyles and social traditions that contain specific meanings are not transcendent.

However, passages that contain specific moral directives are applicable today. The Ten Commandments in the Old Testament are reiterated in the New Testament, and it is still wrong to lie, steal and kill another person.

We must take care not to expand the intended application to fit what might be convenient, or what we want it to mean in order to support a particular theology.

This entire process requires mental discipline.

The term church discipline is not found in the Bible. Matthew 18:15-20 gives direction in resolving wrongdoing only between individual Christians. There are no punitive actions prescribed in Galatians 6:1. 1 Corinthians 5:2 refers to a church-goer who was likely not a Christian.

Correct present-day application of "church discipline" passages likely means the continuity of the pursuit of holiness, accountability, and patient conflict resolution, but the discontinuity of public shaming and removal from fellowship.

WE HAVE FORGOTTEN HOW TO DISAGREE.

Many of us struggle with the notion of discipline today. We just don't like how it sounds or feels. We battle moving past our feelings, and we don't like hearing the word 'no.' So instead of taking on that mantle and exerting the emotional & mental energy required, we glibly pronounce everything healthy or good. To avoid a conflict, we say:

"That's great!"

"You do you."

"I'm glad you're finding yourself"- even if we know it's not great or healthy. We do it because many people aren't comfortable with disagreement anymore. We have forgotten how to disagree. Disagreement often seems to be taken as an assault on our persohood or identity- always personally. It shouldn't be. Disagreement is not hate. Rather, it's a reflection of our value of diversity and mutual respect towards one another.

It's really draining to correct my kids sometimes. Sometimes I just want peace around the house. It's so much easier to avoid conflict and let them have what I know isn't good for them.

DISAGREEMENT IS NOT HATE.

We know what is good for us. No one gets married planning to get a divorce. No one plays a sport and plans to lose. No one invests to lose money. We want to be successful in life. Knowledge tells us what to do. Wisdom shows us how to do it. Discipline does it.

A person of character has all three.

CHAPTER TEN

TERRORIST

This guy wasn't going down without a fight.

My dad and other agents in Cleveland had been tracking Ray "Luc" Lavasseur, a fugitive on the FBI's 10 Most Wanted List, and they received a tip he was hiding out in the Cleveland area. Lavasseur was wanted for murder in the death of a New Jersey state trooper and a suspect in several domestic terrorist bombings. After being estranged from United States policies during his service in Vietnam, he became a member of a revolutionary group called the United Freedom Front, which had designs on overthrowing the United States government. Considered armed and extremely dangerous, this guy was on a mission to change the world, and he didn't mind using violence to do it.

It was a harrowing arrest. While agents were apprehending him, there was a scuffle and at least one agent was kicked in the face (think Jean-Claude Van Damme for you '90s movie fans). Then he was taken to the Cuyahoga County jail to be held for interrogation. That's when the real fun began.

The FBI needed DNA evidence, but Levasseur made it clear he wouldn't cooperate. They could, however, cut or pluck a small amount of hair from Lavasseur to compare with evidence from the scenes of the crimes he was thought to have orchestrated. This was forensic evidence collection. And guess who had the experience in forensic evidence?

You guessed right. Good Ol' John Sommer was nominated to take the lead here. He also knew how to use a pair of scissors, so that meant the job of being the hairstylist fell to him.

But Luc, as he was called, didn't agree he needed a new haircut. Also, he was a combat veteran and dedicated martial artist in top physical condition. He hated the federal government and any authorities connected to it. This was going to be interesting, to say the least.

My dad and three other agents proceeded to an interrogation room, where Lavasseur was held. The door was unlocked by the corrections officer and opened just enough to allow the agents to slip in. Then the door closed shut to the sound of a click. They were locked in now. No going back.

The suit-wearing agents calmly explained to the fugitive they needed to collect a hair sample to use for identification purposes. Nothing crazy, no big deal. It'll take two seconds, and you won't even notice. But before they could finish their monologue, the dude pushed himself back in his chair, and vertical-jumped up onto the table like a participant in the NFL Combine, even though his hands were cuffed.

"Bring it on", he said.

If you've ever been in a fight, it was that moment.

Things turned surreal. It's like you're in a dream watching yourself in slow motion.

That was the moment. The enemies stared, sizing each other up, waiting for the inevitable. Who would make the first move? Ah man. How bad was this gonna be?

Then, they were in it.

Luc descended upon them from the table with astonishing speed. It was all moving too fast to see anything now. Grappling, slapping, and grunting. Agents getting hurt, people yelling in pain, retreating, and jumping back in the melee. The scrum of bodies slammed against the wall, then back onto the table, breaking a leg and sending the whole group crashing to the floor.

And yes, Jean-Claude Van Damme made a cameo appearance starring as Lavasseur, kicking agents in the stomach and the groin as he whirled his body around. Every time someone got close, they got hurt.

More punches, kicks and smacks and after what seemed like an eternity, Luc was in a head-lock while others held onto his arms and legs tighter than Rose held onto Jack in *Titanic*. Before he sunk, of course.

Just a regular day at the office.

Finally subdued, the domestic terrorist spat a mouthful of saliva into my dad's face as he collected the prized locks.

Placing their valuable trophy in a cheap paper bag, the agents knocked on the door for the officer to unlock it and gingerly walked out, limping, and bruised. My dad asked for a towel.

"Hey, you @#%8&s!" Lavasseur called from the room.

The agents turned around.

"I'll see you when I get out of prison!"

They said nothing and kept walking.

Law enforcement professionals, because of the character they are expected to exude, should not react to insults. It's an arduous task, but it's part of the job.

Here's the point: Luc Lavasseur was ready to fight, and he did. It's not that this guy just didn't want his hair cut, he morally opposed the United States government. For him, it was an evil state. Police and the military and prison system officials were an abhorrence to him. They were sellouts, actors of the totalitarian state, oppressors. So when his enemies approached him, he persevered towards his long-term vision. He fought back vigorously to block their goal.

Luc Lavasseur fought for what he believed in.

He didn't give up.

It could have also been self-preservation: don't give them the evidence they want and drag this thing out as long as possible.

He fought because he held strong beliefs that were challenged.

The agents fought, too. Not because they enjoyed getting kicked in the face or threatened. They believed the suspect was dangerous, and they wanted to protect others from harm he might do.

We also must persevere and fight for what we believe in. If you don't believe in anything, there's nothing to fight for. Said differently, if you believe in something, you'll fight for it. And sometimes we do have to fight, even though we may not want to.

That's okay. It's part of life. It's where discipline comes in.

So, here are some questions: What do you need to fight for right now? What makes you pound the table? What makes you vertical-jump onto a table, ready to take on anything that stands in your way?

WHAT MAKES YOU POUND THE TABLE?

For those of us who are married, allow me to suggest one of the biggest places we need to fight is for the health and faithfulness of our marriage. My dad told me he was propositioned several times on his job. During interviews, a woman would make herself sexually available to him, or call later at the office to offer additional information. As far as I know, he never did this.

"What am I gonna do? Leave your mother and you kids?", he answered once when I asked him about a big fight he and my mom were having. It was as if leaving hadn't even crossed his mind, that wasn't an option for him. I remembered that glimpse of resolve and perseverance and think about it when things get hard in my own marriage.

That was exemplary character.

Perseverance means we fight, we struggle to overcome, we keep going.

If you've been married long enough to have moved past the honeymoon stage, you know marriage requires just that perseverance. We must work to understand the other person. We must fight the temptation to be unfaithful or take the easy way out. We must fight to be unselfish. We must swallow our pride and say things like,

"I was wrong."

"I'm sorry."

"Will you forgive me?"

That's not easy to do. It takes discipline and humility and being a secure, self-differentiated person. There are many influences and options that fight against a healthy marriage. Here are two of the most dangerous I've noticed:

Commitment-less relationships, friends with benefits, and open marriages are becoming less stigmatized and gaining popularity as a viable relationship option. The argument is that traditional relationships or marriages can be reimagined, and an additional person (or two) may provide something emotionally and sexually one's spouse cannot. But all we need to do is watch a polygamous reality show to see the jealousy, comparison, and bitterness. Someone always gets hurt. It didn't work well in the Bible, either.

And what happens if the pseudo-commitment ends? What if there are kids involved? Divorce and broken relationships leave painful scars on children.

Pornography is also a problem some today consider normal and harmless if viewed occasionally or ethically. But there is nothing harmless about porn. First, it is nearly impossible to occasionally look at porn. You're either addicted or not addicted. Second, if you are in an intimate relationship, it is simply not possible to look at porn and not experience comparison with your real-life sexual partner. That is not healthy, that's poisonous. Our real partners won't act the same as performers in porn because porn isn't real. It's just that, a performance.

Fight for your marriage by keeping yourself from the traps of unfaithfulness and porn.

Porn produces garbage character.

That's not who we really want to be. If character is who we are when we turn out the lights, I have never heard someone say they were proud of a failed marriage or of being addicted to porn.

At the end of his life, the apostle Paul sat alone in a cold prison cell and penned these words, knowing he would soon be executed.

> *I have fought the good fight, I have finished*
> *the course, I have kept the faith.*
> 2 TIMOTHY 4:7

Paul had fought. He had to fight. The Ancient Near East wasn't thrilled to hear about Paul's Jesus, especially when Jesus was found to be incompatible with other local deities. Jesus was bad for business and culture. Paul had been mocked, socially ostracized, disrespected, arrested, beaten and imprisoned. He was one of the first through the door to tell the world about Jesus.

GOD DOES NOT WANT US TO ALLOW THAT TO HAPPEN.

It's okay if you don't want to persevere. It's okay if you don't want to be a fighter. Fighting hurts. Not everyone is comfortable with conflict and many of us just long for harmony. I wish we lived in a world of perfection and peace and beauty where pushing back and standing firm were not necessary. But we don't and so we need to fight. We just do. It's either that or let evil win. God does not want us to allow that to happen.

When John Sommer carried a revolver, he always loaded the first three chambers with .38 Special. But the last three were loaded with .357 Magnum, an extremely potent round designed for maxium power and expansion. Dad said if he was still shooting after 3 shots, he'd want those last three rounds to be Magnums because he knew he'd be in a fight. .357 rounds end fights.

THE WORLD IS ON FIRE WITH SUFFERING, INJUSTICE AND EVIL.

The world is on fire with suffering, injustice, and evil. Every day, morality and character are being challenged.

If you're a parent, you're

part of another fight. If you have good awareness, you know there's a battle for your kids' hearts going on. And you want to win that battle. You know the answer isn't to just say yes to everything, to give up or throw in the towel. That is less draining, but it doesn't set your kids up for success. That's not how you really want to raise them.

Parenting well is a battle against the negative influences that assail our children, as well as our own selfishness, ipatience and laziness.

Someday, we'll arrive at the end of our life. We will lay in our bed and be given our Ativan and Morphine. Like Paul, we will have finished the course. If we believe in God and that we will live forever with Him in Heaven, we will finally have the peace and paradise we long for. Things will finally be as they should. The world was meant to be a place of joy and beauty. It will be that way again.

But now is not that time.

Right now, it's time to fight.

For more faith-based parenting tips, visit theteachingfather.com

CHAPTER ELEVEN
VICTIMS

When I was a kid (decades before the internet existed) I saw pictures of dead bodies from my dad's work. They were declassified pictures of murder victims and crime scenes. But it wasn't normal back then. Photographs were only available in magazines and newspapers, completely unlike today when you Google something and see just about anything.

And those pictures were real.

I was around nine or ten when I first visited my dad's office. His supervisor had mob victim photos cut and pasted into a macabre collage framed outside his office. The Mafia wasn't known to play well with others. They left many victims in their wake. Often, they were rival outfit members, but some were their own people who talked to federal agents. Being an LCN (La Cosa Nostra) member carried a health risk- significantly shortening your life expectancy.

My dad's boss said the pictures he put up there helped him remember what he was fighting against. I witnessed that gruesome tapestry every time I visited my dad's office, walking faster as I went past. Pictures of mutilated people, decomposed and murdered human beings, blown-up cars, and dismembered body parts.

Okay, the boss sounds a little nuts, now that I think about it.

Later, that same boss was instrumental in helping John Sommer learn more about what following Jesus was all about. At the time, John was still coming to terms with what he believed about God, life, good and evil. Like many of us, he was raised in a quasi-Judeo-Christian culture where Christianity was assumed but not necessarily embraced. My dad's boss Bob introduced him to a real faith and relationship with Christ. Bob did not succeed in getting the Mafia to stop killing each other, but he did help make an eternal impact on my father and our family. Now that's worth making a collage about.

It was a shock to process this information when I first began to see those pictures. The images didn't go away, and maybe that's why I slept with my light on for so long. It took time to go back to playing with Legos and watching Scooby-Doo. Schoolhouse Rock and Super Friends weren't the same, either.

With the lab technician background, my dad was head crime scene analyst in Cleveland- also known as the dead body guy, which was an unsettling and not necessarily sought-after title. Whenever the FBI found a body in the Cleveland area, whatever time or day of the week, he got one of those serious, can't-tell-you-anything phone calls, and then disappeared. He taught police departments and gave slide shows of crime scenes to demonstrate lessons. I am talking about that Jurassic-era circular slide carousel that clicked around and projected each image manually. Later the FBI developed the Evidence Response Team, which is a focused team of agents and technical staff trained in evidence preservation and retrieval. My dad formed and led this team in Cleveland. You'll find these teams on every major crime scene today.

He was assigned to the organized crime squad, which primarily targeted the LCN which was at its zenith in the '50s, '60s, and '70s. These nationally syndicated crime families had a presence in most major cities and made their income through illegal gambling, stolen goods, loan sharking (high-interest lending to people unlikely to pay the loan back), and rackets (an extortion scheme where criminals offer protection to business owners from crimes they themselves commit). A major source of national income for the mob was a skimming racket in Las Vegas, with mobsters requiring a portion of casino earnings.

With the coming of the internet and digital technology, especially surveillance cameras, crime became much less physical. Money could be stolen easily with the push of a button instead of beating someone up with brass knuckles or stealing a tractor-trailer to sell the freight on the black market. Since digital strategies were never a part of the mob's business model, they were not able to successfully pivot to this.

The most notorious Mafia case in Cleveland history was Danny Greene, the infamous and ruthless Cleveland mobster depicted in the 2011 movie, *Kill the Irishman*[7]. John Sommer was interviewed for the accompanying documentary. As an Irishman, Greene challenged LCN for control over the city's rackets. This was not a recommended thing to do. During his ascent to power, Greene became a federal informant, feeding information about rival crime rings to authorities. Maybe this emboldened him to take on the mob. Danny Greene taunted his enemies on local TV during a bloody, years-long turf war where people went missing and showed up stuffed inside of walls or dumped in rock quarries. Sooner or later, everyone wound up dead.

Bad character perpetuates bad character.

One of the mob's favorite ways to get rid of people was by car bomb. It was the preferred method of assassination because evidence was destroyed in the explosion, leaving police and FBI without leads.

After at least two failed attempts on Greene's life, one where the assassin shot and missed, and one in which the lower level of Greene's personal home was bombed, Danny Greene was finally murdered by car bomb in 1977. The bomb was planted under the car parked next to Greene's while he was at a dentist appointment. Even mobsters need to brush. However, the information he provided at the time of his death proved instrumental in crippling the Mafia in Cleveland and it has never recovered. A popular saying in Cleveland was that in life, Danny Greene lost to the mob. But in death, he won.

My dad personally worked the Greene case and subsequent fallout cases from the investigation. During that time and acting on the tip of an informant, one ill-fated mobster named Keith Ritson, an associate of Greene's, was found shot to death at the bottom of a deep, murky quarry. Because of the near-zero visibility and unpredictable contents at the bottom, local law enforcement divers refused to search it. U.S. Navy salvage divers comfortable with diving in dangerous conditions had to be brought in to retrieve the body.

Deep beneath the surface, the darkness was thick. So thick the Navy divers reported afterward they only made it back to the surface by following their own bubbles. As they finally reached the bottom, a diver reached out their hand and touched cold steel. An old hand cart rested on the muddy, refuse-strewn bottom. Chained to it and wrapped in plastic sheeting and electrical wire, was the decompsing body of Ritson. My dad assisted in securing the evidence, and I saw him on the local news working the site.

Months later, another crime scene was found. Agents received a tip someone had been murdered in a tropical fish store on the West Side. After scouring the store for hours in search of evidence such as a murder weapon, hairs and fibers, drops of blood, holes in the wall, or broken furniture indicating a struggle, the FBI came up empty-handed.

Then John Sommer put on his thinking cap. The first floor had original hardwood floors. If someone had been killed, the blood would have seeped down through the floorboards, soaking the plywood underneath. Down the ancient, narrow steps and into the dank, ominous basement they went, and with flashlights in hand, Evidence Response Team members panned the predecessor-of-plywood basement ceiling above their heads. Small circles of light danced wildly in all directions. Creaks from people walking around upstairs.

Stop.

Dad's flashlight focused on a wide dark spot towards the back wall. It was long and contrasted sharply with the lighter color all around it. Someone flipped on the lights, and they drew in for a closer look. Directly upstairs in the same location was a large, dusty, empty aquarium, placed on a rug. The heavy aquarium was moved, the rug pulled back, and bingo. A huge pool and smaller puddles of telltale dried blood that someone had tried to wipe up. This is where it happened. Analysis of the sample wood fiber would confirm the DNA evidence.

Let me say this.

I didn't ask to hear these stories.

They're not encouraging or happy or fun. They're not funny. Listen, I'm a nice, friendly person. I like to be happy and think happy, sunshine thoughts. And when you're a little kid, this kind of stuff is downright terrifying and sad. This creates trauma. Something slowly began to die in me as I heard these stories and watched them play out. Maybe my innocence or naivety. My dad explained that all these people were bad guys, so they deserved what happened to them. That helped a bit, but it didn't take away the shock. I knew it was wrong for people to do those things to other people.

Evil exists in this world. I have met people who denied the existence of God, but I have never met someone who denied the existence of evil. And where evil exists, pain and suffering also are found.

It is good to clarify what we mean when we talk about suffering. Douglas John Hall makes the distinction of two types of sufferings he calls integrative and disintegrative.[8] The idea is simple enough. Hall argues that some suffering is good for us. The suffering and hardship that mold us into strong, well-adapted human beings is a positive thing. Imagine doing a bench press exercise. If you use the proper form and amount of weight and repetition, you will grow stronger. This is integrative suffering. Though there is initial pain, suffering gives way to greater strength and health.

> **I HAVE NEVER MET SOMEONE WHO DENIED THE EXISTENCE OF EVIL.**

But imagine the bench press exercise again. If you use incorrect form, too much weight or repetitions, you can easily strain your bicep tendon or tear your rotator cuff. If that happens, you won't be able to use your shoulder. You will be in constant pain and likely require surgery. This is disintegrative suffering, and this is what we constantly wrestle with today. This suffering leaves us in grief, pain, and death. At least on the outside, there is nothing good about this kind of suffering.

Admittedly, it can be hard to distinguish which type of suffering we are in during the moment, and a great deal of it depends on how we process the suffering.

Job from the Old Testament experienced massive pain and suffering, and a whole lot of it all at once. Out of nowhere, he lost his livelihood, his livestock, then his children, and finally his health. At first, he did well. Hanging in there, processing the change, trusting God, and accepting his circumstances. But then he began to lose heart. He started to become bitter, and he struggled and questioned God and began to despair. His friends offered platitudes and unhelpful advice that made things worse. He did not give up on God, but he was very broken and frustrated.

He was in constant dialogue with God- talking and talking and asking, seeking the reason for his calamitous situation. Finally, God answered Job and provided perspective amid the changes. Frustratingly, He didn't provide the answers Job was looking for. He didn't tell Job why he suffered- even though God knew very well why. Instead, He refocused Job on Himself, the God who is Master of pain and suffering. This helped Job trust again in God's character and put him back on track. Shortly after that, God took away Job's suffering.

God reminded Job of His character.

I would have despaired unless I had believed that I would see the goodness of the Lord In the land of the living.
PSALM 27:13

Pain and suffering are not how things are supposed to be, that's why pain hurts. It's not normal. Evil, pain and suffering were not part of God's original plan. Our angst testifies this is true. But He tells us that someday, He will make it right. In the midst of it we need to have hope that he will.

And He will wipe away every tear from their eyes, and there will no longer be any death; there will no longer be any mourning or crying or pain; all these things are gone forever.
REVELATION 21:4

And we know that God causes everything to work together for the good of those who love God, to those who are called according to His purpose.
ROMANS 8:28

Seeing those dead bodies as a little kid, even though traumatic and evil, also gave me hope. It gave me hope because I knew it was wrong. I knew it wasn't how it was supposed to be, and it made me want to fight back against it.

It started to make me into a fighter.

That's why I became a missionary and minister, to push back the evil and give hope. Having hope that things are going to get better affects how we live. It's that long-term vision that in the end, living and doing and believing what we know is right *will* pay off. We need to have hope that all this will make sense someday, that things will be worth it.

JUSTICE IS RIGHTNESS.

Hope is why we want to be men and women of character. We have a deep longing for justice. Justice is rightness.

Everyone who is mentally healthy knows what right and wrong is. It is disingenuous when we pretend moral right and wrong are relative and up for personal interpretation. That is not true. There are different cultural and temporal nuances, but deep inside we know we are all the same. We are unified, as image-bearers of God, in our true identity and knowledge of truth. We are unified, though we erect barriers to keep each other out and evil tries to tear us apart.

It won't win.

HOPE DRIVES OUR PURSUIT OF CHARACTER.

Hope drives our pursuit of character. If you are a Christian, you believe this. You believe that God will fix this broken-down, mangled, banged-up world. And you are motivated to start living out of that hope right now, today. The Christian life is living like we are already in Heaven. Today.

We got this.

More importantly. God's got this.

And things *are* going to get better.

CHAPTER TWELVE
KIDNAPPING

Amy Mihaljevic was a sweet, unassuming little 10-year-old girl when she vanished in 1989 from a suburban Cleveland shopping center. It was one of the most high-profile cases Cleveland has ever seen. To this day, a suspect has yet to be charged. This unsolved case still haunts Northeast Ohio law enforcement and citizens alike. Her recovered little blue bike stands in the evidence room of the local police department, like a shrine.

She was a middle schooler who loved horses and had good friends. Her home life was sometimes rocky, but whose isn't? Around the time of her disappearance, she had been receiving phone calls from a man claiming to be a co-worker of her mother. Her mom, he said, had received a promotion at work. The man wanted to enlist Amy's help to pick out a congratulations gift for her.

She was last seen being led away after school by a white middle-aged man, his hand resting on her shoulder.

When police recovered Amy's body in a rural Ohio county nearly four months later, John Sommer was the first one called to the scene. Years later when I was an adult, my dad told me about the condition in which her body was found. I won't share it here. Suffice it to say Amy had been sexually assaulted and stabbed to death. Her body, wrapped in a 1960's era homemade curtain made from a bedspread and placed a few yards off the road, showed no attempt to hide her remains. My dad said the killer wanted her body to be found. It was his attempt to "return" Amy's body after he had finished with her- as an act of perverted kindness to the family.

It bothered my dad to work the case because my sister was just a few years younger than Amy. Also, the Mihaljevics lived in our city. In fact closer to our neighborhood. For many reasons, it hit too close to home.

Shortly after Amy's body was found, the Mihaljevics' marriage disintegrated. Amy's mother Margaret was never able to recover from the lack of closure and justice. She developed health problems and the poor woman slipped into alcoholism and depression- eventually passing away.

Many prime suspects were vetted in the early days of the case and even more have been surfaced since. Books have been written with theories about who killed Amy, documentaries have been made, evidence has been collected and analyzed and re-analyzed. Hundreds of people have been interviewed, some polygraphed, some swabbed for DNA evidence.

But no arrest has ever been made.

My dad wrestled with not having a clear resolution to the case. He thought he was better than that. After all, it was a dead-body case, and he was the dead-body guy. He constantly talked about it, fretted over it, frustrated with the outcome or himself, even though it was hardly his fault. He and many other agents and police worked and over-worked themselves for years and

STRENGTH OF CHARACTER MEANS ACCEPTING OUR LOSSES AND FAILURES.

years. Almost 20 years after her abduction, he called a detective working on her case to discuss a new idea he had about connections with the evidence, still piecing things together.

He never let it go.

A few years ago, I received a call from the FBI. They had refocused on Amy's case, but now with advanced DNA identification capabilities. Since my dad had worked with Amy's body, they wanted to exclude any of his DNA accidentally deposited from the profiles they extracted. The FBI asked if they might contact one of my dad's brothers or sisters to obtain a DNA swab. They would be the first choice, and I would be the second. It was sobering and poignant to think I might be called upon to assist in Amy's case. My aunt graciously volunteered to give her sample, but nothing came of the reinvestigation. The case remains open and unsolved.

Sometimes in life, we have to accept failure. That sounds like a platitude, but not everyone fails gracefully. It takes humility and good character to do so. In fact, it is far less common to fail well.

It's been said that humility is not thinking less of ourselves but thinking of ourselves less. That's a big difference, and hard to put into practice. We don't degrade ourselves, rather we recognize that we weren't ever all that in the first place. We have limitations, like everyone does.

HURT PEOPLE HURT.

Many of us have been hurt or wounded in life, and unhealed hurt tends to foster bitterness and jealousy. These toxins can leak out onto others. Hurt people hurt. Richard Rohr profoundly said, "If we don't transform our pain, we will always transmit it".[9]

Pride hides weakness. Humility admits it. We can self-differentiate from our failures when we have a healthy concept of identity. Pride is not a healthy view of our identity; it is a distortion of it. It's an overcompensation for weakness. On the inside, prideful people are the weakest. They are hurt and insecure.

Hurt and insecure people must protect themselves. Like bullies, they beat up on other people to make themselves feel better. Often, they refuse to admit when they're wrong or apologize. They are terrified of letting their weakness show. So they tirelessly manipulate and blame-shift to avoid appearing weak or wrong.

That is ugly character.

We don't want to be weak, but it's good to traffic in reality. So, whether we want to be weak or wrong, we are. Chances are the people close to us know this already. My wife is shaking her head yes. Humility is the ability to admit weakness and still accept ourselves.

HUMILITY IS THE ABILITY TO ADMIT WEAKNESS AND STILL ACCEPT OURSELVES.

Strength of character means accepting our losses and failures, yet still moving forward and forgiving ourselves. If we live long enough, those losses and failures are inevitable. We are constantly changing and change always involves loss. It's part of being human.

David of Israel started well after his victory over Goliath and inauguration as king, but like so many spiritual leaders, he relaxed his discipline and gave in to his sexual desires. I like the word "desires" instead of temptation here, because temptation can have an over-spiritual connotation to it, as if we give in to some outside force of temptation, when we ourselves are responsible for our behavior. After David

CHANGE ALWAYS INVOLVES LOSS.

slept with another man's wife, he ordered the murder of Uriah to cover up his adultery. Then he was confronted by the prophet Nathan. Recall the Bible not only shows us examples to follow, but examples to avoid. Nathan famously stuck his finger in the king's face and said,

"You are the man who has sinned!"

This exposure led to David confessing his sin, admitting failure. Then David said to Nathan,

"I have sinned against the LORD."

Nathan replied, "Yes, but the LORD has forgiven you, and you won't die for this sin (2 Samuel 12:13)."

David probably looked pretty weak and inadequate to

some when he confessed his failure. But they would have neglected to see it actually took tremendous strength of character to admit failure. Maybe that is part of why, despite his wrongdoing, he was called a "man after God's own heart."

For though the righteous fall seven times, they rise again,
but the wicked stumble when calamity strikes.
PROVERBS 24:16

It's not how we start, it's how we end.

My dad struggled with Amy's case. Not that he should've given up, but he had a hard time accepting his limitations. Not being able to give the family justice left a bitter taste in his mouth.

IT'S NOT HOW WE START, IT'S HOW WE END.

But it wasn't the first time Dad had failed. When they found the site of the murder underneath the aquarium, the agents and police began to examine the walls of the store and quickly realized some of them were false, fake walls erected to hide money and drugs in the space between- actually a pretty good hiding place. Dad quickly inspected the walls but did not reach his hand down far enough in between the real wall and false wall to grasp a murder weapon. He concluded the weapon was not there and walked away. Then the police detectives did their inspection, reached down farther in the space between the walls, and recovered a cheap, throwaway revolver stained with dried blood: the weapon. Dad's failure to find key evidence became the subject of a good-natured joke between him and the detectives, yet it was still a failure. He still looked stupid.

ANYONE WHO CANNOT ADMIT FAILURE IS SOMEONE WE SHOULD BE CAREFUL AROUND.

Anyone who cannot admit failure is someone we should be careful around.

That's untrustworthy character.

Those people are not who we want to be. The stripping, breaking power of failure and embarrassment cuts into us, topples our fabricated identities and lays us bare. Bare, real, safe people are those we want to have as our friends. Those are the people everybody likes. In a workplace, everyone knows who the jerk is. They also know who to go to when they need a friend. As we observed earlier, we want to pursue wisdom in life, and wisdom comes from real-life experiences of screwing up, admitting it, and learning a lesson. Pastor John Wimber said: "I don't trust a leader without a limp."[10]

When we accept our failures and limitations, we can give them over to God, declare our dependence on Him, and trust Him for strength to keep going.

Being humble is essential for quality character. And yet, it is so hard, so scary, so uncomfortable to be humble. Simultaneously, humility is so attractive, so winsome, and so admired.

It takes the other aspects of character for the strength to achieve it.

CHAPTER THIRTEEN
DRUG STING

I only saw my dad cry once or twice when I was growing up. Part of it may have been the Boomer, tough-guy persona, and he didn't feel free to cry. But the other part was that he just wasn't a crier. I can relate. I didn't cry when I saw my wife coming down the aisle. That's when not being a crier became a problem. Incidentally, and while we're on the subject, it's very healthy for men to cry and we've come a long way here. Older generations picture an ideal man as stoic, non-emotional, showing no weakness. But people don't follow stoicism. They follow passion. They follow authenticity. We're learning now that you can still be a dude and cry. If you own it, it actually means you're more secure and strong, not weak. Men, cry if you need to.

PEOPLE DON'T FOLLOW STOICISM. THEY FOLLOW PASSION.

Dad teared up when we put my first dog to sleep. Other than that, I honestly can't remember ever seeing him cry.

Until now.

A massive FBI sting operation had just occurred in Cleveland. Just about an hour earlier, the local five o'clock news had broken the story, along with pictures of numerous suspects. They were law enforcement officers. A staggering forty-four police and corrections officers from five different agencies across Northeast Ohio had been arrested. They were accused of providing protection for cocaine shipments being flown into the city.

Drugs coming into cities follow an observable distribution route that can often be predicted. FBI agents posing as drug dealers made initial contact with a county corrections officer who was happy to help make sure coke got into Clevelander's hands for a quick cash payment of five hundred dollars. He also brought along some of his buddies, which included other corrections and police officers. As word got around, the list of officers who wanted in swelled and people began to come out of the woodwork. Finally, the ringleader had to tell new officers there was no more room.

So a waiting list was made.

The officers did more than just provide protection. They assisted in loading and unloading the cargo of illegal drugs as shown in the surveillance videos. These people knew exactly what they were doing as they piled the packages into cars and vans, and they did it willingly, uncoerced. Tragically, an officer scheduled to work one night was forced to apologize when he showed up late. He was supposed to protect a plane delivering fifty kilograms of cocaine, but the D.A.R.E. (Drug Abuse Resistance Education) program he was leading at a local elementary school ran long.

He arrived in the department's D.A.R.E cruiser.

That is despicable character.

It was the largest public corruption case the FBI had seen nationally up to that date, and my dad was the Supervisory Special Agent. A sickening tragedy for the city of Cleveland.

That night, John came home and went straight into the family room where I was watching TV. I was in my early twenties at the time, just graduated from college and living at home.

With tears welling up in his eyes, he came over and hugged me.

I'm thinking, What are you doing, man?

Then he explained. Many young men my age went to jail that day, and he had been a major part of making that happen. These young men ruined their lives with dumb decisions- for a few easy bucks.

"I'm just grateful you weren't one of them," he said.

I was puzzled.

"Uh, okay, yeah. Thanks," I said, and went back to whatever I was doing.

I didn't consider myself to be in the league of the type of guys who had gotten arrested, or even at risk for that behavior. What they had done would have never crossed my mind.

But to my dad, I wasn't that far off. I was a young man, like them. I could have been going to prison for twenty-five years like they were. My dad was grateful, thankful, sorrowful for what he had to be a part of. By the way, how many other planes flying drugs in did they miss before this? How much sorrow transpired before this case?

Law enforcement traffics in sorrow.

It cleans up after it. Sometimes it produces it.

Even when you know you're doing the right thing, it still hurts to see what you have to see and do what you have to do. That sorrow and trauma can cling to you and poison your relationships- unless you have a way to set it down and let it heal. I won't go into fully how to do that here, but the main thrust of it involves a word I've used before: self-differentiation.

Self-differentiation is a psychological term for the process of separating our experiences from our self-concept. With the trauma found in law enforcement, this means creating a cognitive and emotional separation between yourself and the crimes and criminals you experience. It also means positive self-talk (a form of cognitive behavioral therapy), reminding yourself that you really are helping people by the job you do. Finally, it means believing that the criminal world is not how things are supposed to be. It's wrong. We can heal even more if we believe someday God will make everything right.

THE CRIMINAL WORLD IS NOT HOW THINGS ARE SUPPOSED TO BE

For my dad, the trauma of sending so many young men

to prison helped him realize how much he cherished his family. He and the other agents worked tirelessly for close to a year gathering evidence, and now the bad guys were going to jail. The case was solved. It was closed, but the human fallout was just about to begin. Now wives, girlfriends, parents, and kids would pay the price. They were about to be stung as well, even though they did nothing wrong.

Thankfulness. A counselor once told me the cure to discontentment is thankfulness, gratitude.

I do come home and hug my kids and wife most days, but not every day. Sometimes I'm grumpy and irritable. I act like they are getting in my way, preventing me from doing what I really want to do. That is painful to admit, but maybe you can relate. Yes, that's human nature, normal to a certain degree, but I don't like that. I don't want to be selfish and not value what's most important.

THE CURE FOR DISCONTENTMENT IS GRATITUDE.

I can be a jerk. My wife is shaking her head yes, again.

I didn't go to jail that day as the forty-four drug ring protection suspects did. I was still in my dad's life the next day, but what does it take for us to begin to cherish what's most important in life? Do we actually need to go to prison? Do we really need to lose our job or health or money?

I think of the Israelites in the Old Testament. Time and time again is the theme.

Time and time again after they left Egypt for Canaan, the promised land, God met them with miraculous signs and provisions. He parted the Red Sea. He provided food. He allowed them to be victorious in battle. He kept their clothes and shoes from wearing out. When they wanted meat, He got them meat. When they needed water, He got them water. But time and time again, Israel turned their back on

God. They whined and complained. They weren't thankful. They even asked to go back to Egypt to become slaves again because the journey was too tough. They gave up on Moses when he left to get the Ten Commandments. They came up with their own god instead.

I can't judge them because, even though I'd like to think I'm better than they were, I'm afraid I would've done the same things. Just like Adam, I would've eaten the forbidden fruit. I'm a complainer and whiner, too. It's because I feel entitled. Time and time again, I am ungrateful.

FBI agents do a lot of shooting to practice and prepare for worst-case scenarios. They are required to qualify, or pass a shooting test four times per year to maintain proficiency.

My dad used to take me to the FBI range when I was in middle school and high school. It was at an Army base on Lake Erie. Agents were qualifying there all week during the late summer, and afterward, there was time for recreational shooting. That's when my dad brought me.

I loved going to that range. It was a long trip out there, and my dad and I would spend quality time talking about things we enjoyed. Those times were special to me, I can picture them now. On a beautiful summer day when we got to the range, I'd carry my ammo over to the bench and shoot for hours. Other agents started to come around, talking and laughing with my dad. It was like a big party. He introduced them to me, and I was always given a warm and friendly welcome. These positive interactions with other agents were part of being raised by the FBI. I was like royalty, and all because my last name was Sommer.

Then the good stuff: agents offered me other guns to shoot (Um, yes, please!): Uzis, old-style M-16s, fully automatic Thompson Machine guns, MP-5s, .44 magnums, sawed-off shotguns. All sorts of really neat stuff for a teenage boy to shoot.

I understand this might give some readers pause- the idea of providing a bunch of guns for your son or daughter to shoot. Firearms are not for everyone. Many people are uncomfortable around guns and that's entirely understandable and reasonable. At the same time, I would argue that practicing responsible marksmanship in a positive, safe, social setting is a far healthier, real-world experience than sitting alone in a basement, staring at a screen, and killing people in a video game. Or going out and drinking underage, like most kids did at my school.

You see, what my dad did was give me a better reality, a better story. It was a tremendous confidence-builder for me as a young boy to feel comfortable around firearms and improve my marksmanship. I learned wisdom that I pass on today to my kids and many others.

One time the range closed early.

That was a problem for me.

My dad and I had gotten there late and were only able to shoot for about a half-hour. As a middle-schooler, the son of an agent, and an experienced summertime FBI range shooter, I was angry. This was my time to shoot. I deserved it. So, I decided to go and tell the principal firearms instructor just that.

I had heard of this man. He was a big guy and former Marine. Dad said he once split his shirt like the Incredible Hulk when he flexed for everyone on the squad. That would have been an interesting day at the office. I wonder if that was a reimburseable work expense.

After looking around the range for a while, I found the instructor standing in the shoot house. I had to look up at him when I spoke and I can't remember my words exactly, but I remember his. He glared down at me through his Aviator sunglasses and huffed,

"Stay out of my underwear."

Then he walked away.

I wasn't sure exactly what that meant, but I figured it was along the lines of I wouldn't be shooting anymore that day. It embarrassed me, hurt my feelings, and then made me steaming mad.

Another nearby agent observed the interaction between the instructor and me. He called me over while he cleaned his gun. He explained that coming to the range was not a right, but a special privilege. He said everybody liked my dad, and most people would never get the chance to do what I got to do. I needed to be grateful for being invited.

I thought about those words and chewed on them as I sulked. I was still mad, but they made perfect sense. I knew he was right. It was a seminal moment for me.

Being grateful is good character.

The firearms instructor could have been more kind and patient in his response, but I also realized I was wrong. I should have been more grateful.

What I learned was that over the years of coming to the range and having the run of the place, I became entitled to certain things. I felt entitled to shoot for as long as I wanted and I failed to realize it was a privilege, not a right owed to me.

A person of character is an unassuming, unpretentious person. A grateful person.

Gratefulness is the key to contentment. Many things in life stifle our gratefulness. We expect the air conditioning to work in the summer, the car to start when we turn the key or push the button, the lights to turn on, the internet to be fast. That's okay and completely reasonable, but sometimes these things don't work and that is super-annoying. That's what happens when we become accustomed to certain things and maybe feel entitled to them. When they are taken away, some people call them "first-world problems."

When our expectations are not fulfilled, we become angry. Again, that is normal and understandable, yet that is also a warning sign in our hearts to remind us to be grateful. We have so many blessings if we stop and think about it. We don't all have the same blessings, and we're not all blessed in the same manner, but I do not believe there is someone who isn't blessed in some way. The very fact we have been born and given life is a blessing. Every heartbeat is a blessing. Every breath is a blessing. Every hot shower, every good cup of coffee, every meal, every enjoyment. People are a blessing. Family is a blessing. Health is a blessing. Being able to run is a blessing.

Find a quiet place, go for a walk, and bring a journal to take notes.

First, write down certain areas in your life where you are frustrated or discontent or angry or feel wronged. Then begin a list of everything you can be thankful for. Keep it going, add to it later and throughout the day. Throughout the week.

I bet you'll keep adding. Then, thank God for those blessings. Be grateful and thankful.

Then pass that thankfulness on. Give back, as they say.

The cure for discontentment is gratitude. A person of character is thankful.

CHAPTER FOURTEEN
JUST DAD

Have you heard people talk about how meaningful it was when their mother or father attended their sports games growing up? Have you sensed the hurt from someone who didn't receive their parents' time or approval? It's painful to hear. There's a deep, lasting scar. Sometimes an open wound. Like we observed previously, hurt people are likely to hurt others.

My dad was the second in his family to graduate from college and receive a bachelor's degree. He worked hard, paying every penny himself. Every summer and during breaks in classes he was working at my grandpa's meat stand at the West Side Market or LTV steel or somewhere else. The day he finally graduated from Ohio State University, his father was not in attendance.

That hurt my dad deeply.

How do I know this? Because he told me. He told me on the way to one of our hunting trips. There was pain and bitterness, even years after. He never forgot it.

We connected meaningfully that time in the middle of the night on the highway, driving to our hunting grounds as I clutched a hot cup of caffeine with both hands. This was the humility part of good character, My dad showed weakness but still remained comfortable in his skin.

Children spell love: T-I-M-E.

I called my dad at the office about a million times during his career. I still know that FBI number by heart. 216-522-1400. His secretaries knew my name. I had a special pass. There was a standing order to the two

CHILDREN SPELL LOVE: T-I-M-E

squad secretaries to patch through any call from his wife or kids. That was a short list and it made me feel special. As far as I know, my dad always took a call from me when he could.

He may not have been able to talk long at times, but I always knew he was glad I was a part of his life. That communicated my value and priority over his work. I was first, work was second.

On another nighttime car trip, Dad told me about one of the most difficult moments in his career as an FBI agent.

I WAS FIRST, WORK WAS SECOND.

He and his partner had just arrested another mob member and were leading him away in handcuffs to be imprisoned, possibly for the rest of his life.

This man was different though, he had a family with young kids. The FBI conducted another early morning raid, thankfully less eventful than others. The man's wife and several of his kids awoke in the commotion. They stood, staring in the doorway as agents walked the suspect out of his house in handcuffs. His wife stood in silence, but as they stepped into the yard, his young son decided to fight for what mattered to him. Bursting into tears, he ran after his father in footed spider-man pajamas and clung to his father's leg.

"Daddy, Daddy, Don't leave! Don't leave!"

With a lump in his throat, my dad kept walking with the suspect, tugging harder with the added weight of a broken-hearted little boy.

He never forgot that moment, either.

I can imagine that taxed and challenged Dad's character, but he knew it had to be done. That little boy's relationship with his dad changed forever that day. Time together was no longer an option.

We only get one shot at parenting our children. And our kids only get one mom and dad. We need to make our time count. As I said previously, John Sommer was by no means perfect, but one of the things he did best, one of his greatest legacies, was to engage with me on my level. Today I try to do the same thing myself on my kids' level. For me, that means chasing my kids around, pretending to be a monster, and acting crazy.

"Daddy, chase me!" one of the kids will shout.

I morph into a zombie, complete with a dragging foot and gnarled hands, growling and limping towards my kids. Other kids on the playground join in, saying,

"Chase me too! Chase me too!" squealing with delight as the zombie closes in.

I'm pretty sure this is one of the things God put me on this earth to do.

Suddenly, I've enlisted an army of little boys and girls ready for a better story. They gang-rush me, jumping on my back. Ten little ones all over me, hoping to bring me down. I'm getting tickled, hung on, pummeled by tiny fists. Finally, they succeed. With a loud crash, the zombie goes down and breathes his last.

Or does he?

The zombie-fighters cautiously tiptoe towards the silent menace. Closer...closer...closer...

"ARRRRRRRRRRRRRRRRRRHHHHHHHH!"

The little fighters scatter, screaming for joy.

Oops, my glasses just got scratched.

I guess I should've employed wisdom and took them off before I started.

One time my oldest son got embarrassed when I transitioned on a beach and began chasing some of our friends' kids around.

"Dad, do you really you have to do that? That's kind of embarrassing."

"Ryan," I said. "Don't you remember how much you loved it when I chased you around when you were a little boy?"

Though we don't know for sure, I bet Jesus was the kind of guy to chase little kids around the playground, too.

One day some parents brought their children to Jesus so
He could lay His hands on them and pray for them. But
the disciples scolded the parents for bothering Him. But
Jesus said, "Let the children come to Me. Don't stop them!
For the Kingdom of Heaven belongs to those who are
like these children." And He placed His hands on their
heads and blessed them before He left.
MATTHEW 19:13-15

The disciples were Jesus' bouncers. Like a celebrity, He needed protection and management (though not really protection). So, when several little children were brought to him, the disciples' attitudes soured.

Great, more work for us, they thought.

Jesus was too important for these kids. His time should be spent on more significant peo-ple- people who really mattered.

We know for sure the disci-ples tried to drive the moms and kids away because, in that culture, kids were the responsibility of their mothers or other women, but not

JESUS WASN'T A NORMAL JEWISH MAN.

Jewish men. Men had more pressing things to do than in-teract with kids. Children were viewed as irrational adults in the ANE- more liability than asset. More mouths to feed, and little in return, until they got older.

But you know what I love about Jesus? You know what's so great? He was not a normal Jewish man. The guy broke stereotypes everywhere he went! Let's think about it:

First, He stopped what He was doing and rearranged His Google calendar. He allowed His agenda to be changed. Then, He picked up a toddler and placed her on His lap, a gesture of affection and acceptance. He used her as a living object lesson. Lastly, He put His hands on them all and blessed them.

I'll bet that was a good blessing. Those kids lived special lives after that, I'm sure of it.

Do you think that little girl smiled when He sat her on His lap? Can you imagine the other little ones crowded around, hoping to be accepted, too? Dirty little faces, hesitant smiles, bare feet, hoping to sit on His lap?

Do you think Jesus smiled?

Incidentally, since we're talking about breaking stereotypes and fighting for what's right, do you want to be a real rebel, a real revolutionary, a culture-changer, a fighter for social justice, someone who breaks the rules and puts people first, a person of gritty, real, down-to-earth, powerful character? Do you want to make a difference, do you want to love people, heal them, help them, spend your life on what matters most?

Are you ready for a better story?

Then Jesus is the guy you want to follow.

Remember this: Jesus did not receive any coolness points from His interactions with women and children and lepers and tax collectors from the professional religious people. He only earned their anger. But He didn't come for them.

THEN JESUS IS THE GUY YOU WANT TO FOLLOW.

Don't be afraid to get down on the ground, act like a fool, and chase your kids around. It doesn't even matter what you do, just as long as you spend time with them. Take a kid with you wherever you go: the hardware store, swim practice, the nursing home, your workplace. Bring them into whatever you do. They will remember forever how you smiled, laughed, and showed your approval to them. You may even bless some other kids along the way.

Then, be genuine and tell them about your victories and

failures, your joys, and hurts. Apologize when you need to and ask for their forgiveness when you are wrong. Build their character with your character.

Good character perpetuates good character.

Give your kids the gift of confidence and acceptance that comes with having a secure relationship with their father and mother.

Give them time.

CHAPTER FIFTEEN
RETIREMENT

The late Catholic priest Henri Nouwen said we try to find our identity in three illegitimate sources. It goes like this:

1. I am what I do (career)
2. I am what I have (belongings, experiences)
3. I am what other people say about me (image, reputation)[9]

The Fraternal Order of Police is the police officer's union. A sticker on your car window indicates you are a member.

My dad had three on his.

He purchased the FBI's issue firearm for himself when he had to turn in his own.

He got a special deputation from the Cuyahoga County Sheriff and the U.S. Marshals.

To stay connected to law enforcement, he volunteered to conduct dangerous surprise tractor-trailer searches with the Marshals.

My dad retired from the FBI in 1999. When he did, I could see he struggled.

He had lost his superpowers. His badge and gun disappeared. Sure, they let him keep his credentials, but the word, R.E.T.I.R.E.D unmistakably punched smack in the middle doesn't hold the same weight. Gone was the identity of John B. Sommer, FBI Supervisory Special Agent, Organized Crime Squad. He had become just a regular guy again, the guy he was thirty years prior. Being in the FBI was one of the things my dad was most proud of in his life.

That is probably hard to take. When you've lived something, when something has been your normal for so many years, change is hard. Especially when your identity is as fraught with significance as a law enforcement officer. The essence of carrying a badge and gun is by nature exclusive and unique. You need to have a special authorization to carry them, and most people are not authorized.

But what is our true identity as men and women? Who are we after we retire? Are we still significant? Do we still matter or are we simply a forgotten, throw-away person?

I can't emphasize this point enough. In our American culture, we assign massive, massive amounts of significance and identity to our vocation. Human beings are made to worship and give themselves to something. We are made to praise, long for, and pursue beauty. In The Brothers Karamazov, Fyodor Dostoyevsky writes that more than anything in life, we strive for someone (or something) to worship.[10]

I would make a slight edit to this.

You know, since I can capture a principle in writing better than Dostoyevsky...

I would say more than anything in life, we strive for someone to *please*.

So, putting the two together, we try to please ourselves by worshipping work and our work identities. In fact, though we often joke about wanting to retire, I have perceived an underlying shame for many that accompanies retirement. Some believe they are now seen as unimportant and obsolete. Others become bored, not knowing what to do with themselves or how to occupy their time, This is difficult because as people, we need to feel like we're significant. Work is where we look for it. Work is the location where we face challenges and achieve success. Workplace success is how we feel like we matter.

Let me be clear: God created work, and work is good. Working hard is honorable, and achieving workplace success

WORK IS NOT WHERE WE SHOULD LOOK FOR OUR TRUE IDENTITY.

is an important goal. But work is not where we should look for our true identity.

There was a man years before we were born who tried to do just that. A man who thought he could please himself and acheive happiness by doing work. By the way, most of what is in the Bible is people trying the same things we are trying today. That's what makes it so relevant and timeless.

This man shot for the moon and tried to find identity and lasting significance in his career and accomplishments. His name was King Solomon of ancient Israel and here is his story:

I undertook great projects. I built houses for myself and planted vineyards. I made gardens and parks and planted all kinds of fruit trees in them. I made reservoirs to water groves of flourishing trees. I bought male and female slaves and had other slaves who were born in my house. I also owned more herds and flocks than anyone in Jerusalem before me. I amassed silver and gold for myself, and the treasure of kings and provinces. I acquired male and female singers, and harems as well— the delights of a man's heart. I became greater by far than anyone in Jerusalem before me. In all this, my wisdom stayed with me. I denied myself nothing my eyes desired; I refused my heart no pleasure. My heart took delight in all my labor, and this was the reward for all my toil. Yet when I surveyed all that my hands had done and what I had toiled to achieve, everything was meaningless, a chasing after the wind; nothing was gained under the sun.

ECCLESIASTES 1:4-11

King Solomon sought to please himself, and though he tried vigorously, was not able to achieve the significance and contentment he hoped for. It continued to slip away from him, like the wind.

My dad reached the zenith of his FBI career. I watched the Attorney General of the United States and FBI director personally commend him for his service. He shook the hands of two presidents. He was the supervisor of a renowned organized crime squad in Cleveland credited with the deconstruction of the Mafia. He oversaw many successful cases and retired with the respect of his colleagues and a healthy, comfortable pension for life.

But this is where wisdom comes in, and we need to get this right. We need to know just who we are and our purpose in life. The Bible tells us our purpose is clear.

You shall love the LORD your God with all your heart and with all your soul and with all your might.
DEUTERONOMY 6:5

God is the One we want to please.

A few years ago, I ran into a retired agent my dad worked with. I asked him if he was enjoying his retirement. He talked my ear off for half an hour telling me he'd rather work fifteen hours a day than be retired. He was bored and depressed. I wonder how he is doing now.

"You can only watch so much TV," he said.

"YOU CAN ONLY WATCH SO MUCH TV."

Then I talked to another agent. I asked him the same question. His answer was the exact opposite.

"Yes! I love retirement. I'm done with guns and badges. In fact, I'm sure there's another guy who has taken my place and doing my job just as well, probably even better. I'm re-modeling my kitchen and Beth, the grandkids are coming next week, right?"

It blew my mind to juxtapose these two perspectives. I marveled at this man's strength of confidence and character that allowed him to properly locate his work. He had let go of the work idol. His life didn't depend on his work. Sure, it had been significant and meaningful, but it ended. That's not all there was to him. He had more going on, more to do and be. It didn't define him anymore and he was okay with that.

It's healthy and normal to want to be good at what we do. We wouldn't be healthy if we didn't. Ambition is a good thing. But if we value personal or professional greatness most, there will forever be a nagging doubt in the back of our minds that we need to do more, that we should be more.

When we retire, it will be: *should have* done more, *should have* been more.

Personal greatness is fleeting.

Speaking of personal greatness, and since I already shot myself in the foot with the professional Christian comunity, it may be time to rethink how we do church in our post-Christian, post COVID Western world.

We're learning a lot from COVID, in particular. We're learning that we can (and must) do church without big buildings and multi-campuses or even physical attendance. We're learning church isn't the only place Christians can receive biblical teaching. Podcasts can now do that very well. As church leaders, we need to stop asking the question: "How can we get people to come back to our worship services?" Instead, we should ask: "What is God doing now?"

I know that might sound really scary, but perhaps God is calling us to let go of some of our traditional ideas about how to do church and simply redirect our focus back to people. People are the church- not our brand, our strategy, our worship services or our brick and mortar. If there are no people, there is no church.

Churches and ministries should not exist to perpetuate themselves. They should exist because God changes lives and wants to change even more.

We name our children because we have the authority to do so. We declare who they are.

WE NAME OUR CHILDREN BECAUSE WE HAVE THE AUTHORITY TO DO SO.

In the same way, we need someone else with greater authority to declare our identity and significance to us. A baseball team cannot declare itself the World Series winner, only the baseball commissioner can. We cannot confer an academic degree upon ourselves. A board of directors does. The Person who has the authority to say who we are and the power to back it up is the Maker and Creator of people. The One who wrote the owner's manual. He informs our character, and this Maker is not just an entity. This Maker is a being. The being to whom most of us pray. God.

God declares us significant. And being a child of God is where we find our greatest identity and purpose.

Being a child of God makes me want to be a man of strong character, because that's who I am on the inside. I know this, and I want to be congruent with my true identity. We all do. I want to be a good man, husband, and father because I was made to do good.

I felt bad for my dad when I watched him flailing and still grasping for the law enforcement identity that had ended. I never got the chance to talk with him about it, but I saw it from a distance.

I also learned wisdom by watching his struggle. I learned that everything in life eventually changes, dies, breaks, runs out, leaves, or comes to an end.

Nothing has illustrated this concept more vividly to me

than being a hospice chaplain.

Most patients in hospice were young once. They were full of life and vitality. They were strong of mind and body. They picked out paint colors for their bedrooms and took vacations.

But things changed.

Now they are incontinent of bowel and bladder. They use sippy cups. They wear bibs while someone else feeds them pureed green stuff.

WE NEED SOMEONE WITH GREATER AUTHORITY TO DETERMINE OUR SIGNIFICANCE.

Does it matter if their adult diapers accentuate their figure? Do they make fashionable catheter bags?

The goal of life is not to avoid being fed by someone else. It's to have peace in our hearts when we are.

Everything changes.

Everything except my real identity, which continues long after retirement.

I am a son of God. Loved, accepted, and delighted over. Yes, delighted over.

I am made to do good and push back evil.

I am made to be a man of character.

This identity lasts.

CHAPTER SIXTEEN
LEGACY

January 28, 2009. Blizzard-like conditions in Northeast Ohio. White-out. Massive snowstorm.

The entire Cleveland area had been dumped on by four feet of snow in just two hours. A winter storm advisory was in effect. No one was going anywhere soon in the whole region that day. I had just woken up and gone downstairs. I turned on my coffee maker and started our wood-burning stove.

Our two little boys were still asleep. I powered on my flip phone inside the black faux leather case and saw I had received a voicemail. Interesting. Voice mails never came in that early.

I listened to it and heard my aunt's somber voice telling me my dad had collapsed and been taken to the hospital. At the same time, our home phone rang. My mom was calling. She labored hysterically to tell Emily the same thing as she rode with Dad in a separate ambulance to the hospital.

I threw on some clothes and was out the door and on the way to the hospital in ten minutes. Just before I left, my wife pulled me aside and told me through tears,

"I just want to tell you... that I love you and you're my hero."

Emily was thirty-nine weeks pregnant- almost ready to give birth. It sounded like my dad had had a stroke or heart attack. Thoughts raced through my mind as I began the long trek across the Cleveland metropolitan area to the West Side, over quiet, cushioned, snow-padded highways. The roads were completely covered with packed snow, and almost deserted. I cried a little, prayed, and called some friends for prayer support. The weather was dangerous as I drove around thirty miles an hour the entire way to the hospital. Then the news started to sink in. At first, I reasoned that it probably wasn't that bad. People survive heart attacks all the time. That does happen.

But then I realized how serious it could be. People die from heart attacks all the time.

When I arrived at the hospital, I pulled at the heavy door and wondered if I was at the right place. I was hoping I'd be told my dad wasn't even there, that this was all a dream. I glanced at the sitting area as I walked and saw a man in a suit wearing an FBI badge. It was the head of the Cleveland FBI.

I was at the right place.

And it wasn't a dream.

Then I was ushered to the intensive care floor and told the news. I was the first one through the door to visit him after my sister and mother.

My dad purchased a new Ariens snowblower and he was thrilled. This thing was a beast, and he couldn't wait to use it. Powerful snowblowers are coveted things to have in the Cleveland area. He especially loved that it had a headlight.

After excitedly blowing five neighbors' driveways in a row, he went inside to sit down. He wasn't feeling well, he told my mom. Shortly afterward, he suffered a massive heart attack. He recovered briefly, long enough to knock the phone out of my mom's hand when she told him she was calling 911 (He didn't think it was serious), but soon became unconscious again as the squad arrived. He was immediately brought to the hospital and underwent successful stent surgery. Later, I learned he was revived several times in the ambulance and was probably without oxygen for well over five minutes.

This was not good.

I was allowed in to see him.

I cannot find the right words here to describe what it was like walking into the room. Those of you who have experienced a loved one in this situation can help me explain the feeling:

A punch in the stomach and face at the same time. A sickening, staggering feeling. Light-headedness. Surreal and dream-like. Crushing sorrow.

That's all I can say.

I could not take in what my eyes were seeing. There was my dad, wearing that dumb hospital dress, hooked up to tubes, ventilator down his throat, beeping, flashing, signaling devices. I wanted all that junk to be taken away from him. Just let him be normal again.

He didn't talk. He didn't open his eyes. This was my strong dad I've looked up to all my life. He was always healthy and capable. He beat me at arm wrestling and threw me around the pool as a kid. I had never seen him like this. I had seen people in the hospital in this condition before, but never dreamed one day it would be my dad.

"You know, this doesn't mean I'm going to carry your tree stand into the woods for you," I quipped.

I thought I saw him try to respond. I really did. A hospice nurse once told me hearing is the last thing to go in a dying patient.

That night the drugs that kept him sedated were removed. That was when he should have regained consciousness, the critical moment, but he did not. Nothing changed. It slowly started to dawn on me that he may not be coming back.

The days passed and my father's condition remained the same. No progress. Meanwhile, Emily's due date came and went. We were going to have a baby very soon. I constantly checked my phone, listening to voicemails.

At one point, after some visitors left, I entered the visiting room alone. I looked around to make sure no one else was there, then knelt on the floor and wept profusely for five minutes.

Damn. My glasses were all spotted up afterward.

I learned that your eyelashes flip tears up onto your glasses when you cry.

Finally, I got a call from my wife telling me she had begun having contractions. Dejected, exhausted and in shock, I left my dad's hospital bed and went home to take Emily to our son's hospital. On the early morning of February 5th, my special and wonderful son Jack was born.

I spent all that day with Emily and my new son. The next day, I woke up and drove back to my dad's hospital. I felt as if in a dream. I was transitioning from a place of new life, hope, and joy to a place of death and sorrow and loneliness.

After ten days of being unconscious, MRIs, and CT scans, the doctor pulled us into a private room and explained my dad's condition. We already knew it: he was brain-dead and beyond healing capabilities. His heart functioned well, but the lack of oxygen had permanently damaged his cognitive abilities. If he ever woke up, the doctor assured us he would not be the same person we knew. He showed us a recent scan, showing no neurological activity.

My sisters and mother began crying quietly. I just sat there in disbelief. The decision was made to remove supportive devices once we all had a chance to say goodbye.

After this was done, I started to walk out of the room, knowing it would be the last time I saw him alive. I needed to get back to my family, to my son, to life. So I looked at my dad, recited a recent joke we had laughed about, and told him I'd see him soon.

Then I left.

I got the call in the early morning from my sister. John Sommer passed away on February 7, 2009.

For those of you who have lost a loved one, this will sound familiar.

I immediately found myself launched into a place of shock, sadness, anger, and depression. I was in a fog for about six weeks, like I was watching myself from outside my body. I lost my appetite and didn't feel like eating, but the generous and kind people from Hudson Community Chapel kept bringing meals over. I didn't want the winter to end because that meant time wasn't standing still. It was moving on, without my dad.

During alone times, I questioned my character and what I was doing. Why did I want to be a good person anyway? I mean, what's the point? And why did I want to be a minister? Just to appear successful and obsess over numbers? Was it even about God or was it really just all about me?

I wrestled hard with God. I was angry and felt wronged by Him.

At some point during the spring, my brain broke through the haze, and I begrudgingly accepted God's will, realizing I'd rather live with Him and be confused

I'D GONE GODLESS BEFORE, AND THAT WAS EVEN WORSE.

and angry than go it alone without Him. I'd gone godless before, and that was even worse. I wasn't going back there.

Joseph of the Old Testament lived a unique life of faith, hardship, and redemption.

He started from a privileged background, as his father Jacob's favorite son. That was the first problem: the father played favorites. If you are a parent, never do this.

His father gave him an expensive, multi-colored robe. This made him appear significant and stand out over those who wore the everyday cream color of wool and linen clothing. Jacob did not do the same for his other sons. On top of this, Joseph earned the ire of his brothers by shooting off his mouth and making foolish statements. He was given several dreams from God, but instead of using discretion, he flaunted his gifts and special knowledge.

Joseph needed character growth.

So powerful became the hatred of his brothers that

they sold their half-brother into slavery in an approaching caravan. Afterward, they casually sat down to laugh it off and eat a meal. That's how callous they had become.

There's a lot of bad character in all of that.

But God wasn't finished with Joseph.

He became a slave in the house of an Egyptian official but was quickly promoted to manager. Joseph was an attractive young man. This guy was ripped, intelligent and most attractive of all, honorable. He soon drew the attention of the officials' wife. One night she propositioned him. As a punishment for refusing her advances, Joseph wound up in prison where he stayed for several more years.

LIFE IS BETTER WITH GOD.

But throughout all this, Joseph clung to God. He grew through integrative suffering into a man of strong wisdom and character. His relationship with God remained intact.

Because life is better with God.

When you have a baby, you normally stay for a few days in the hospital afterward to make sure everything's okay.

The food isn't very good. The carrot slices are serrated. The Jello has pieces of fruit embedded into it.

The nurses ignore you if you're the husband and you barely get any sleep because you have to stretch out on that crummy pull-out chair/couch vinyl thing that is always too short.

As a man, I know I have no room to complain.

Finally, after a couple of days, they hand you the baby to go home. That special bracelet that corresponds to the baby is clipped off. Then they place the baby in the mother's arms as she sits in a wheelchair. You wheel your wife out of the hospital with a mixture of anxiety and joy and with something you didn't have when you came in. A baby.

Your baby.

They give you the baby because it's yours. It doesn't belong to anyone else. It's not the hospital's, not the nurse's or doctor's, it's yours.

Look, she even has your eyes.

You'll get an adult-sized hospital bill in a month, but you get to keep the baby.

This makes sense because the parents are the ones who care the most about the baby. There is no one on earth that loves the baby more. He or she is in the best hands it can be.

After a while, the baby begins to understand this. The mother and father provide sustenance and care. The baby begins to trust.

We can begin to trust, too.

You see, we belong to God and His hands are the best place for us to be. And God isn't finished with us yet, either.

Joseph was released from prison and given a place of honor and responsibility. He was entrusted with saving the lives of millions during a terrible famine. His life was redeemed.

GOD ISN'T FINISHED WITH US.

In time, God showed me the blessing of the timing of my son's birth. He used my suffering to refine my heart and character. Losing my dad will always hurt, but I can see some redemption in the pain, as well.

God wasn't finished with Joseph and if you're breathing, He isn't finished with your life, either.

We've all been raised by someone. Take an honest look at how you were raised. We have become believers in some things. Other things were shoved down our throats and we are recovering from them.

That's okay. That's normal.

Now as adults, we can choose whom we want to be and how we want to live our lives. We can continue to keep the script we were raised with, or we can choose to *rewrite* the script.

Let me say that again. If you still have breath, you can rewrite the script.

> *The Lord's mercies never fail. They are new*
> *every morning. Great is your faithfulness.*
> LAMENTATIONS 3:22-23

In the first chapter, I defined good character as kindness, respect, courage, discipline, gratitude, perseverance and humility. Ask yourself to what degree your life reflects these virtues.

WE ARE ON A CHARACTER JOURNEY- INFORMED BY OUR SPIRITUAL JOURNEY.

It's okay to come as you are. Jesus made that clear during His ministry. We are all on a character journey that is informed by our spiritual journey, which consists of what we trust and believe in. Jesus taught people how to have the greatest, most significant, joyful, and adventurous journey of all— follow Me and become My disciple. He provides our moral foundation and example of character to follow. If we want to improve our character, following Jesus is the place to start.

At my dad's memorial service, one of his longtime friends and colleague, stood up to eulogize him. He shared some nice things, called my dad "John Sommers" instead of Sommer, even though he knew him for thirty years. But the most significant thing he said was this,

"Hell, even the bad guys liked John."

Later, another agent met with a Mafia informant who knew my dad. The agent told him that John Sommer had passed away. The informant wept.

Amazing. Even the bad guys cried.

Shoot, I better start crying.

My dad and his job taught me character. The bad guys could see it too. And that character was a catalyst to something even more significant than self-actualization: A relationship with God.

I say relationship because it's not a set of dos and don'ts. It's not a stuffy, cheesey, boring religion with an irrelevant, angry and out-of-touch God.

I'm not interested in that.

It resembles more a human relationship, a connection with a person. That relationship with God helped show me my brokenness and limitations. It helped me see how much I wanted and needed to change on the inside.

I began to despise my selfishness and dishonesty and began striving to be a man of character. To do that, I knew I needed God in my life. In following God, there is a reason for living and an adventure to live. Love God, love others. That was something big enough to be worthy of my life.

The world is on fire with evil and injustice. We are the firemen. Jesus is the living water that puts out the fire and heals our hearts. The FBI is a signpost of justice, character, and goodness. A symbol of who we really want to be on the inside. But the FBI is imperfect, it falls short. The only one who can truly match this ideal is Jesus.

Along this journey of character, we're gonna blow it. None of us are perfect. Look at the examples of those from the Bible, and there are even more.

Adam blame-shifted, Noah got drunk, Abraham trafficked, Sarah snickered, Rebecca plotted, Jacob lied. Joseph bragged. Moses murdered. Rahab was a sex worker, Gideon panicked, David was unfaithful. Samuel and Eli were crappy fathers, John the Baptist ate bugs, Peter couldn't swim, Martha stressed out, Mark peaced-out, Thomas doubted. Paul persecuted, Philemon was a slave owner, Timothy was nervous, the apostle John?

Well, John wasn't too bad.

None of these people were finished. God still used all of them greatly. Give yourself grace. Acknowledge your failures and ask for forgiveness from those you've wronged. Then keep moving forward. Keep getting back up. Fight for what's right.

But don't do it alone. Build up allies in the fight for character. Stack the deck in your favor. Surround yourself with people you want to be like. Seek God. Be humble and honest. Learn wisdom and apply discipline. Be grateful. Give away your time.

"I'm not finished with my faith yet," my dad said in the fall of 2008 while we were driving back from the shooting range. We had just sighted in our guns for deer season. His last season, unbeknownst to us. He got a nice deer.

Four months later, he *was* finished with his faith. On earth, at least.

But his faith continues through those in whom he invested his life, his family, his friends, his co-workers.

And me.

I am continuing his faith through this book.

And now, I pass it on to you.

To all of you who knew John Sommer, I know he would have been so excited for you to read this. Not because *he* was so great, but because he tried to represent Someone *greater* in his life.

Someone with perfect character: Jesus.

So here is my attempt to give a final charge John B. Sommer would approve of:

We belong to God, and He isn't finished with us yet. Jesus wants to heal the evil and brokenness inside us. Then, He wants us to be the first one through the door to push back the evil and heal our broken world.

Blessings to you on your journey.

If this book has given you some things to think about, or raised any questions, or if I can be of assistance to you in any way, I'd love to hear from you. Just send me an email.

raisedbythefbi@gmail.com
SCOTT SOMMER

FBI mourns hard-working agent

Posted by John Caniglia/Plain Dealer Reporter
February 23, 2009, 01:47AM

John Sommer spent the 1980s chasing the Mafia out of Cleveland, the 1990s fighting public corruption and, in recent years, coordinating Ohio's drug war. At each step, his colleagues say, Sommer exuded integrity, class and a never-ending work ethic. The man who was quick with a joke and eager to help died Saturday, Feb. 7. He was 62.

FBI agent John Sommer

Days earlier, he suffered a heart attack after snow-blowing five neighbors' driveways.

"That's John," said Ronald Bakeman, who runs the major drug unit in the U.S. attorney's office in Cleveland. "That's the kind of person he was."

A memorial service was held Sunday at Bay Presbyterian Church on Lake Road, where hundreds of his friends in law enforcement showed up to honor the man.

Sommer worked 29 years with the FBI before retiring in 1999 to become the director of Ohio HIDTA – the High Intensity Drug Trafficking Area – a congressional initiative that tracks illegal drug trends in the state's largest counties.

During Sommer's tenure, HIDTA helped seize more than 70,000 kilos of marijuana, 5,000 kilos of cocaine, 364 kilos of methamphetamine, 157 kilos of heroin and 82,000 hits of Ecstasy. The agency also helped in taking $117 million in assets. At the agency, Sommer pushed a simple concept: He made agencies report in detail what they were doing, a move that would prevent the embarrassment of one police department from arresting another's undercover officer.

"He wasn't an in-your-face kind of guy," said Frank Figliuzzi, director of the FBI in Cleveland and the chairman of HIDTA. "He was a behind-the-scenes guy who made quiet suggestions and worked closely with people."

Sommer made his name as an FBI agent during the mob wars. He investigated the car bombing of Danny Greene, a slaying that sent several top mobsters to prison. He also worked the case of underboss Angelo "Big Ange" Lonardo, whose work as an informant helped lead to the dismantling of Mafia families in Cleveland and across the country. And he tracked evidence in the unsolved murder of Amy Mihaljevic, the 10-year-old girl from Bay Village who went missing and was later found dead. Her killer has never been found.

In 1995, he became the supervisor of the Cleveland FBI's organized crime squad. One of his first cases involved an undercover investigation that sent 51 police officers and jail guards to prison for selling their badges for a few hundred dollars. The probe involved an FBI agent posing as a mobster who hired law enforcement to protect phony drug deals. It remains the largest police corruption case in the FBI's history.

So, after seeing everything that he did, how did he keep going?

" My faith has sustained me," Sommer told The Plain Dealer in 1999. "I just never forget who I'm really working for. My priorities have always been God first, then family, then people, then my job."

Sommer graduated from Ohio State University in 1969, planning to become a teacher until a fraternity brother told him that FBI agents earned $10,000 a year. He joined the FBI in 1970 and became a shoe print and handwriting expert. He then spent nearly three decades as a case agent and supervisor.

"He was an agent's agent, who was loved and respected by everyone who ever worked with him," Figliuzzi said.

Another agent summed up Sommer's career: "Hell, even the bad guys liked John."

New Agent and New Son!
Image: Sommer family

**Sledding 1975
(Wait, is this an
undercover pic?)**
Image: Sommer family

Hunting together, 2006
Image: Sommer family

First Big Deer! 1998
Image: Sommer family

Goofing Around
Image: Sommer family

Teaching the Younger Generation!
Image: Sommer family

Grandpa
Image: Sommer family

**Dermatological
Researcher and Inmate**
Image: Temple University Libraries

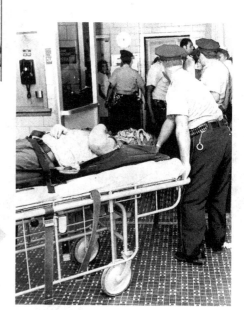

**Injured Guard from
the Prison Riots**
Image: Temple University
Libraries

**Angelo Lonardo
Mugshot, Cleveland OH**
Image: City of Cleveland
Police Dept.

Miami FBI Shooting Newspaper Article
Image: The Miami News

Lonardo Testifying Behind a Screen
Image: The Miami News

The Carnage Afterward...
Image: The Miami Herald

An Agent's Blown-out Car Window from Platt's Mini-14
Image: Miami-Dade Police Department

Bloodied Trunk from the Suspects taking Cover

Image: Miami-Dade Police Department

Agent Dove's Disabled Firearm

Image: The Miami Herald

Luc Levasseur Wanted Poster

Image: Federal Bureau of Investigation/fbi.gov

Domestic Terrorist Bombing, 1970

Image: AP/Marty Lederhandler

Danny Greene

Image: Plain Dealer Historical Photograph Collection

Greene's Car after the Bomb Detonated

Image: Cleveland State University

Unidentified body taken from quarry

Associated Press

COLUMBIA STATION — Navy and Cleveland police divers pulled a body weighted by manhole covers from an abandoned quarry north of this Lorain County community Friday, the FBI said.

The agency refused to speculate on the identity of the body, but a spokesman said the search was part of an investigation into illegal drug trafficking and organized crime in northern Ohio.

FBI spokesman John Dunn said the body was taken to the Cuyahoga County coroner's office for examination and identification.

quarry near Lagrange, also in Lorain County.

Ritson, 32, disappeared in 1978, shortly before he was to go on trial in Cuyahoga County on charges of conspiracy and cocaine sales.

DUNN refused to comment on reports that authorities were led to the quarry by convicted drug dealer Carmen Zagaria, who plea-bargained on several murder charges in federal court in Cleveland last week.

Zagaria is expected to testify in trials against six other men charged with operating a drug ring in northern Ohio that had profits of $15 million a year.

Part of a Local Newspaper Clipping: Victim Discovered in Quarry

Image: The Akron Beacon Journal

An Abandoned Quarry near Cleveland

Image: Cleveland Quarries

Amy Mihaljevic, 5th Grade
Billboard in the Cleveland Area, 1989

Image: WKYC studios

Amy's Body is Found,
February 1990

Image: News 5 Cleveland

SUSPECT IN ABDUCTION

BV9890713

VICTIM: **AMY MIHALJEVIC** · Age 10
          628 Linford, Bay Village, Ohio

SUSPECT: White Male · Age 30-35
          5'8" - 5'10" tall, medium build
          Dark hair, possibly curly, with bald spot top/rear
          Trace of beard growth
          Possibly wearing round glasses and a tan jacket

THERE IS A REWARD OF UP TO $13,000 for information on the whereabouts of Amy Mihaljevic and the identification of her abductor. These two artist's depictions are recollections of two different witnesses.

CALL BAY VILLAGE POLICE: CALL FBI:
871-1234   **522-1400**

BIBLIOGRAPHY

[1] Sutin, Lawrence 2014. *Do What Thou Wilt: A Life of Aleister Crowley*. St. Martin's Press: New York, NY

[2] Adapted from *Becoming a True Spiritual Community: A Profound Vision of What the Church Can Be*. Crabb 2007

[3] Goodman 1988. *Studying Prison Research Experiments: The Balti-more Sun*.

[4] Lubasch, Arnold H. *Ex-Mob Leader Tells of Slaying Father's Killer*. The New York Times, Sept. 24, 1986

[5] *In the Line of Fire: The FBI Murders*. Echo Bridge 1988

[6] Calhoun, Adele Ahlberg 2015. *Spiritual Disciplines Handbook: Practices That Transform Us*. IVP Books Downers Grove, IL

[7] *Kill the Irishman*. Anchor Bay Films 2011

[8] Hall, John Douglas 1987. *God and Human Suffering: An Exercise in the Theology of the Cross*. Fortress Press: Minneapolis, MN.

[9] Rohr, Richard 2018. *Transforming Pain*. Center for Action and Contemplation. https://cac.org/transforming-pain-2018-10-17/ Accessed 11/21

[10] Schroder, Glenn 2020. *Never Trust a Leader Without a Limp: The Wit and Wisdom of John Wimber, Founder of the Vineyard Church Movement*: Thomas Nelson: Nashville, TN

[11] Nouwen, Henri 1993. *Being the Beloved* sermon. Garden Grove, CA

CPSIA information can be obtained
at www.ICGtesting.com
Printed in the USA
JSHW010756030523
40981JS00005B/67

9 780578 358659